M000192026

BIRTH

PASTORING FOR LIFE

Theological Wisdom for Ministering Well
Jason Byassee, Series Editor

Aging: Growing Old in Church
by Will Willimon

Friendship: The Heart of Being Human
by Victor Lee Austin

*Recovering: From Brokenness and Addiction
to Blessedness and Community*
by Aaron White

BIRTH

THE MYSTERY

OF BEING BORN

JAMES C. HOWELL

Baker Academic

a division of Baker Publishing Group

Grand Rapids, Michigan

© 2020 by James C. Howell

Published by Baker Academic
a division of Baker Publishing Group
PO Box 6287, Grand Rapids, MI 49516-6287
www.bakeracademic.com

Printed in the United States of America

All rights reserved. No part of this publication may be reproduced, stored in a retrieval system, or transmitted in any form or by any means—for example, electronic, photocopy, recording—without the prior written permission of the publisher. The only exception is brief quotations in printed reviews.

Library of Congress Cataloging-in-Publication Data
Names: Howell, James C., 1955– author.
Title: Birth: the mystery of being born / James C. Howell.
Description: Grand Rapids: Baker Academic, a division of Baker Publishing Group,
    2020. | Series: Pastoring for life: theological wisdom for ministering well | Includes
    bibliographical references and index.
Identifiers: LCCN 2019031838 | ISBN 9781540960832 (paperback)
Subjects: LCSH: Conversion—Christianity. | Birth (Philosophy)—Miscellanea.
Classification: LCC BV4916.3 .H69 2020 | DDC 248.2—dc23
LC record available at https://lccn.loc.gov/2019031838

ISBN 9781540962737 (casebound)

Unless otherwise indicated, Scripture quotations are from the Revised Standard Version of the Bible, copyright 1946, 1952 [2nd edition, 1971] National Council of the Churches of Christ in the United States of America. Used by permission. All rights reserved worldwide.

Scripture quotations labeled KJV are from the King James Version of the Bible.

Scripture quotations labeled NIV are from the Holy Bible, New International Version®. NIV®. Copyright © 1973, 1978, 1984, 2011 by Biblica, Inc.™ Used by permission of Zondervan. All rights reserved worldwide. www.zondervan.com. The "NIV" and "New International Version" are trademarks registered in the United States Patent and Trademark Office by Biblica, Inc.™

Scripture quotations labeled NRSV are from the New Revised Standard Version of the Bible, copyright © 1989 National Council of the Churches of Christ in the United States of America. Used by permission. All rights reserved.

Chapter 5 quotes from Madeleine L'Engle, "First Coming," in *The Ordering of Love: The New and Collected Poems of Madeleine L'Engle*. Copyright © 2005 by Crosswicks, Ltd. Used by permission of WaterBrook Multnomah, an imprint of Random House, a division of Penguin Random House LLC. All rights reserved.

Chapter 8 quotes from Madeleine L'Engle, "The Risk of Birth, Christmas, 1973," in *The Weather of the Heart*. Copyright © 1978 by Crosswicks, Ltd. Used by permission of WaterBrook Multnomah, an imprint of Random House, a division of Penguin Random House LLC. All rights reserved.

In keeping with biblical principles of creation stewardship, Baker Publishing Group advocates the responsible use of our natural resources. As a member of the Green Press Initiative, our company uses recycled paper when possible. The text paper of this book is composed in part of post-consumer waste.

20   21   22   23   24   25   26   7   6   5   4   3   2   1

Contents

Illustrations

Series Preface

One of the great privileges of being a pastor is that people seek out your presence in some of life's most jarring transitions. They want to give thanks. Or cry out for help. They seek wisdom and think you may know where to find some. Above all, they long for God, even if they wouldn't know to put it that way. I remember phone calls that came in a rush of excitement, terror, and hope. "We had our baby!" "It looks like she is going to die." "I think I'm going to retire." "He's turning sixteen!" "We got our diagnosis." Sometimes the caller didn't know why they were calling their pastor. They just knew it was a good thing to do. They were right. I will always treasure the privilege of being in the room for some of life's most intense moments.

And, of course, we don't pastor only during intense times. No one can live at that decibel level all the time. We pastor in the ordinary, the mundane, the beautiful (or depressing!) day-by-day most of the time. Yet it is striking how often during those everyday moments our talk turns to the transitions of birth, death, illness, and the beginning and end of vocation. Pastors sometimes joke, or lament, that we are only ever called when people want to be "hatched, matched, or dispatched"—born or baptized, married, or eulogized. But those are moments we share with all humanity, and they are good moments in which to do gospel work. As an American, it feels perfectly natural to ask a couple how they met. But a South African friend told me he feels this is exceedingly intrusive! What I am really asking is how someone met God as they met the person to whom they have made lifelong promises. I am asking about transition and encounter—the tender places where the God of cross and resurrection meets us. And I am thinking about how to bear witness amid the transitions that are our lives. Pastors are the ones who get phone calls at these moments and have the joy, burden, or just plain old workaday job of showing up with oil for anointing, with prayers, to be a sign of the Holy Spirit's overshadowing goodness in all of our lives.

I am so proud of this series of books. The authors are remarkable, the scholarship first-rate, the prose readable—even elegant—the claims made ambitious and then well defended. I am especially pleased because so often in the church we play small ball. We argue with one another over intramural matters while the world around us struggles, burns, ignores, or otherwise proceeds on its way. The problem is that the gospel of Jesus Christ isn't just for the renewal of the church. It's for the renewal of the cosmos—everything God bothered to create in the first place. God's gifts are not *for* God's people. They are *through* God's people, *for* everybody else. These authors write with wisdom, precision, insight, grace, and good humor. I so love the books that have resulted. May God use them to bring glory to God's name, grace to God's children, renewal to the church, and blessings to the world that God so loves and is dying to save.

Jason Byassee

Acknowledgments

More than any book I've ever written, the writing of this one has felt like a crowd of people pressing all around my computer, talking, advising, laughing, embracing, and crying as we worked together. I asked moms of all ages to tell me their stories. They obliged, with humor, delight, sorrow, nostalgia, regrets, and gratitude. It was fascinating indeed to talk about this with my own mother and with the mother of my three children. I owe them literally everything that matters in life.

I asked doctors, nurses, and midwives to tell me about their craft, and they gave me stories and much emotion as well. Paul Marshburn, Clay Harrell, Steve Eyler, Kathryn Chance, and many others taught me much and impressed me with their love for their work and their people. My niece Liz Stockton helped me understand midwifery, and Meliea Holbrook introduced me to the gift of the doula.

I read lots of books and blogs, pondered novels and films. The many endnotes in this book are not mere citations but little thank-you notes to theologians, anthropologists, sociologists, and novelists who feel to me like great friends, although most I've never met.

I would tell random people in line at the grocery store or in the next seat on an airplane what I was writing about, and I never wished I'd kept it to myself. All these friends, family, coworkers, acquaintances, and total strangers have made this book what it is. I'm the reporter, the assembler, the docent.

I owe much gratitude for this project and in my personal and professional life to my longtime friend Jason Byassee, whose wide reading and keen intelligence are matched by a compassionate heart. Melisa Blok and Dave Nelson have been warm, responsive, generous, and exceedingly helpful throughout the editing process.

Heidi Giffin; Laurie Walden; my wife, Lisa; my daughter, Sarah; and too many others to name read or listened to me read portions or all of the manuscript when it was rough. They made it smoother, wiser, clearer, and more humane. The amazing Meg Seitz swooped in late in the game and waved her magic editorial wand over the entirety of the book and made it far more compelling.

Introduction

When I was asked to write a book about birth, I hesitated—being a guy, of course. But then ideas and people and stories and wonderment flashed through my head. As a writer, I've never had such an adventure in researching and writing: the privilege of hearing so many extraordinary, wonderful, and tragic stories; stumbling upon so many startling realizations; and gaining a renewed sense of the glory that is God and the marvel that is my life and yours. Moms, midwives, doctors, theologians, novelists, bloggers, and even children have staggered me with their wisdom, experiences, and griefs.

All life transitions inevitably define us, shatter our illusions, or confirm our deepest convictions. But not everyone gets to graduate or marry or retire. We all die, yes, but you can reflect on your death only in advance—or it's someone else's death you grieve. Being born: now that's everybody's experience. We were all born. And what transition could ever be as astounding, risky, gleeful, downright mystifying, and yet entirely natural as birth? And where might we discern the mystery of God's grace, mercy, and purpose more profoundly than in the real miracle and yet mundane commonplace that is birth?

Pediatrician Mark Sloan, in his informative, fascinating, and funny book *Birth Day*, explains how stunning this greatest of all our transitions in life actually is: "There is no time in life, not even the moment of death, that can compare to the human body's transformation in the first five minutes outside the womb. Birth is about radical, creative,

1

life-affirming change. It is about adaptation on a nearly unbelievable scale. Abrupt, rapid-fire transitions are the order of the day: dark to light, warm to cold, wet to dry."[1] Skin color morphs from blue to purple to pink or brown in just moments. Desperately, the child does what she must, what she hasn't been taught, and what she needs to survive the next minute: she breathes.

And there's a cry, the first of many to come in a lifetime of crying out in pain, despair, or even joy. This cry is the most welcomed, eliciting from those who hear it not concern but relief. Anthropologist Wenda Trevathan calls the first cry "the birth cry": "This cry, qualitatively different from all others he will make, initiates interaction, and is the first vocal statement, 'I exist!'"[2]

Your being born makes other people nearly drunk with delight or jittery with worry. Never will you be the subject of so many "oohs" and "ahhs," or maybe panic or tearful laughter. Never again will you be the object of such focused attention. You are never more loved than in the moment of birth. You are never closer to God than in the moment of birth. You are never more like God.

Typical and Exceptional

You are never more like all the other hundred billion people who have ever lived on earth than in the moment of birth. And you have never been more unique, more you, more like the proverbial snowflake or fingerprint. No one has ever shared the peculiar twists and turns of your DNA, even if you are a so-called identical twin. As the geneticist Adam Rutherford points out, "You are both typical and exceptional."[3]

Typical and exceptional theologically: you, like every person ever born, including those born while you've been reading this page, are mysteriously, invisibly, but indelibly imprinted with the image of God. And yet even that image, the one God planted deep within you, is exceptional. God's relationship with you (even if you've not been attentive to it) has its peculiarities. God's unfathomable genius can handle all this endless particularity. God is unfailingly attentive at every moment to each one of us special, but garden-variety, human persons.

Science and theology know you are special. But the stories! When I began research on this book, I started asking moms to tell me their birth stories. Each one, without exception, would get a little wide-eyed and begin by saying, "Well, my story is unique . . ." I thought, "Yeah, yeah." But indeed. Each story really is unusual. And never brief. Ask a mom about the birth of her child, and you'd best settle in; it'll take a while. In *Anna Karenina*, it took Tolstoy three chapters to narrate the birth of a son to Kitty Shcherbatsky, and entirely from the perspective of Levin, the dad, who was fretting outside the door; he wasn't even in the room! Tolstoy movingly rendered the distortion in the sense of time, the disbelief at the casual attitude of those who aren't suffering, and the terror, and then the awe, that are part of childbirth. But what unfolded in there for Kitty? What range of sensation and emotion did she endure? How many pages would that story require?

Having a child: What else can make you feel so special and important? And yet it's something billions of women have pulled off successfully. Even Neanderthals experienced birth. The Australopithecus Lucy, one of the most sensational archaeological finds ever, was some prehominid's child. Right now, human moms, chimpanzee moms, and dolphin moms are having children. People, cows, and bugs are being born. Such a lovely solidarity with others and all of creation. An individual being born: hardly a microscopic blip on the radar of all that transpires on our planet, much less in the universe. And yet, as Thoreau quite rightly puts it, "Every child begins the world again."[4]

Abiding Astonishment

To understand the value of birth, imagine our world as a world with no children. P. D. James did just this in her dystopian novel, *The Children of Men*—which envisions the world in the future, with no children being born anywhere due to mass infertility. This civilization without children turned cruel, despairing, and violent. Part of people's outrage was over the failure to figure out the cause: "We are humiliated at the very heart of our faith in ourselves. For all our knowledge, our intelligence, our power, we can no longer do what the animals do without thought."[5]

For all our ingenuity and scientific advancement, there will always be some residual astonishment and the sense that life's origin eludes our control. When it comes to what we might call the amazement factor—awe, wonder, a summons to reverence—nothing can match birth. When I asked a recently retired obstetrician how he felt about his life's work of delivering babies, he blushed, got a little teary, and fumbled to say how mystifying and wonderful each birth had been. I'm not generally at a loss for words, but after our first child was born, when I attempted to report the news to my mother-in-law in the waiting room, I gasped; nothing but an unintelligible stammer came out.

Our best wordsmiths help but still fall short. Carl Sandburg: "A baby is God's opinion that life should go on."[6] William Wordsworth: "A child, more than all other gifts earth can offer, brings hope with it, and forward looking thoughts."[7] Celeste Ng, in *Little Fires Everywhere*, a novel whose plot features most of the themes we'll cover in this book (birth, infertility, adoption, abortion, surrogacy, and death), penned these words:

> To a parent, your child wasn't just a person: your child was a *place*, a kind of Narnia, a vast eternal place where the present you were living and the past you remembered and the future you longed for all existed at once. You could see it every time you looked at her: layered in her face was the baby she'd been and the child she'd become and the adult she would grow up to be, and you saw them all simultaneously, like a 3-D image. It made your head spin. It was a place you could take refuge, if you knew how to get in. And each time you left it, each time your child passed out of your sight, you feared you might never be able to return to that place again.[8]

Awe. Mystery. Remembering and reflecting on birth will take us to a place of dumbfounded wonder. We modern, practical, controlled, fearful, and often superficial people need to go there, and maybe linger a while.

Stone Age people or medieval people or even my great-grandparents had to have been utterly puzzled and awed by the mystery and miracle

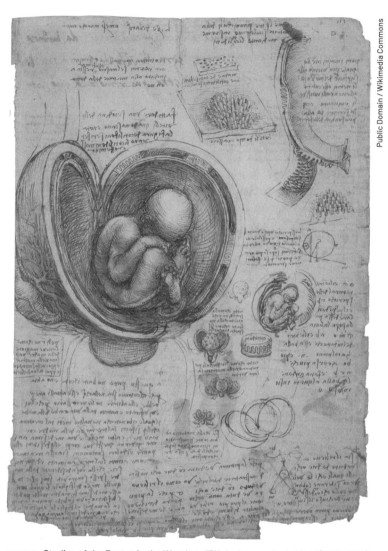

Public Domain / Wikimedia Commons

FIGURE 1. *Studies of the Foetus in the Womb*, c. 1511, by Leonardo da Vinci (1452–1519)

that is birth. Today we may have even better cause to be stunned, since we know more about the mind-boggling anatomical complexities that somehow happen in the womb. We now have stunning photography of fetuses in utero. Before that, the best glimpse of pre-birth life could

be the ink and red chalk drawing of a fetus in the womb, which the
dazzler Leonardo da Vinci concocted back in 1510 (see fig. 1)—an
anatomically detailed, artistically ingenious presentation that Walter
Isaacson described as "purely divine. . . . It captures the human condition with a spiritual beauty that is at once unnerving and ennobling.
We can see ourselves embodied in the wonder of creation: innocent,
miraculous, mysterious."[9]

Seeing ourselves—and seeing God: I hope you will join me in the
adventure I've been on while researching and writing. I've come to
understand me—what and where I once was, and where others have
been too—and the fragility, resilience, normalcy, and miracle that is
life. And of course, how God is there with us. The psalmist traveled
back in time and down in size to recall the glory of being:

> Even the darkness is not dark to you,
> . . . .
> For you did form my inward parts,
> You knit me together in my mother's womb.
> . . . .
> You know me right well;
> My frame was not hidden from you,
> When I was being made in secret, . . .
> Your eyes beheld my unformed substance. (Ps. 139:12–16)

My dream is that this book will lure you into such a posture of stam-
mering praise and awestruck self-awareness.

PART 1

OUR MYSTERIOUS BEGINNING

ONE

In My Mother's Womb

God's knitting: Is that how I got into my mother's womb in the winter of 1954? Is that how you got started? What made the psalmist ponder his own past, when he was a microscopic next-to-nothing, and chalk it up to God? "You knit me together in my mother's womb" (Ps. 139:13). We can say he was inspired, of course. But it's complicated, isn't it? Read novels, watch movies, or listen to your friends or your own life: how you took up residence in utero is a mix of falling in love, testosterone, estrogen, the chance of timing, the proverbial backseat. When and how were you conceived?

My parents were "trying." My own first daughter was a bit of an accident. Lisa and I had just gotten married and moved and taken new jobs—and somehow hadn't gotten around to talking about having children yet. Not long after what must have been conception, we both got a series of immunizations in a clinic with sternly worded signs threatening pregnant women with dire consequences. When the gynecologist gave us the news, I didn't feel joy so much as numbness. We weren't "ready" (whatever that means). We've always called our daughter "the most loved unwanted child in history."

The theologian Hans Urs von Balthasar speaks of "the terrible accidentalness of sexual causation," which may elicit a "reserved awe on the incomprehensible linking of God's creative act with the accidental generation of nature. God did not, so to speak, will him unconditionally;

instead, God connected his own creative act in the light with quite dark and blind co-causes."[1] Your parents: co-causers! Maybe Forrest Gump's words at Jenny's grave fit: "I don't know if Momma was right or if it's Lieutenant Dan. I don't know if we each have a destiny, or if we're all just floating around accidental-like on a breeze, but I think maybe it's both. Maybe both is happening at the same time."[2]

God made me. God made my daughter. God made you. But then you have to say God made all the accidental ones, and you have to grapple (as we will later) with God apparently not planting a little one in the womb of the woman desperately eager to become a mom. God made me and you, and Jesus in Mary's womb; and God made that scandalous child in Bathsheba's womb; and God made those with health challenges we'll ponder later on. When God made the universe, circumstances were put in place for mammals to come into being with this peculiar potential for male sperm to invade female space to create life. How odd of God to knit you and me together in this quirky mix of creation, good intentions, luck, surprise, and delight!

You Really Are Special

The biology of God's knitting is dumbfounding. You and I began as a miracle, a microscopic merger, an outright freak of nature that happens more than four times every second worldwide. Twenty or more were conceived while you read that last sentence. You might blush if you ponder the sexual act that spawned you. But let's zoom in on that moment and what happened: an ovary released an egg, which sailed through the fallopian tube like a wide receiver running downfield ready to catch a ball if thrown. Sperm, exiting your father's testicles, swam upstream through the vagina into the uterus. One out of a spurt of millions of sperm met up with that waiting egg. As Adam Rutherford explains, "On contact, that winning sperm released a chemical that dissolved the egg's reluctant membrane, left its whiplash tail behind, and burrowed in."[3] This penetration, unseen, initiated the transformation of the egg into an embryo, which found its way to the lining of the uterus, coalesced there, and cell division commenced at a rapid pace.

We know things the psalmist never imagined. The chromosomes in the sperm and egg are shuffled, producing a deck never seen before, never to be seen again. You think you are a complicated, complex person? You have no idea. Your genome, the totality of your DNA, has something like three billion coded letters. Each massive batch is utterly unique, even though over one hundred billion people have been conceived and born on earth. Even if you are an identical twin, you're still peculiar. The instructions built into these genes are, at that moment of conception, already directing how you will be constructed, how tall you'll be, the color of your eyes, your proclivity to disease.

Your DNA, by the way, was forged inside your grandmother—as the egg that you came from was made inside your mother's ovaries while she was inside her mother.[4] I never met my maternal grandmother, who died before I was born. We have a few grainy black-and-white photos of her; when I study them, it's a bit mind-boggling to think I once resided inside this woman, Estelle Comer Marley.

Even more humbling, gratifying, and stupefying is the far larger genetic truth—that you descended (in the "great leap forward") from a group of great apes that existed many thousands of years ago. And your ancestry extends even further back into the mysterious origins of life and the universe itself. The psalmist writes,

> When I look at your heavens, the work of your fingers,
>   the moon and the stars that you have established;
> what are human beings that you are mindful of them?
>   (Ps. 8:3–4 NRSV)

Knowing that those stars were billions of years in the making, and that we are too, we have even greater cause than the psalmist to be dumbfounded.

Utterly Dependent

The fused zygote begins doubling in size every few hours as it settles into its new abode in the uterus. After a week, this complex marvel is one-tenth of one millimeter long. Barely there. But talk about a growth spurt: he's twice as long in just one more week; she's grown sixteenfold by week eight, when mom finally figures out she's pregnant. From the fetus's perspective, mom is a colossus, the child downright Lilliputian. Rapid development of the child's fledgling organs and limbs continues for months until mom is showing. After a few more weeks, mom's belly is quite obvious, continuing to expand until it sticks way out there, beautifully if laughably. After a big meal we say, "My stomach might pop." A pregnant woman's looks and feels like it just might, but it never does.

The very early division, compression, and metamorphosis of cells is amazing. Mom, as host, is keeping this new, microscopic life alive with zero effort or awareness. The child isn't exerting effort either. A fragile ecosystem somehow develops, and it actually works. The placenta, really just a temporary organ, provides oxygen and blood to the fetus, sharing nutrients from mom's system, and transferring fetal waste back through mom's body for disposal. Mom breathes, involuntarily, and her oxygen makes its way into her bloodstream. In its aquatic, squishy world, the baby can't breathe, so the placenta functions as its lung.

The umbilical cord shares in these labors. We speak of "navel gazing," with derisive connotations; but where better to look to contemplate the befuddling fact of existence? Mark Sloan, pondering what that belly button once was, points out that "it's just been there collecting lint ever since. But there was a time when it was the center of my world, the sole port through which every molecule of food and oxygen that went into making me arrived."[5]

I love the moment in the film *The World according to Garp* when Garp, despairing that no one is buying his novel, learns that Helen is pregnant. Moved to tears, sighs, and laughter, he climbs onto the bed, uncovers her belly, draws a face with a marker, and says, "He's in here, right? It's nice in there, I know."[6] How good of God at the very outset, before anybody knows you exist, to engulf you in such a nice, nurturing, free-of-charge, secret, and warm world of what can only be called grace.

A Glimpse into the Womb

When I took up residence in my mother's womb, no one knew who or what or how I was until I came out. When it came time for me to become a father, we were afforded a glimpse into the womb, but only by a kind of trickery: the ultrasound, developed to detect icebergs and submarines, provided not a straightforward snapshot but a grayish, grainy impression of a very real creature only a few inches tall. Parents see these images and become giddy, their wee one posing for the first of countless photos—though the child really has nowhere else to be.

I recall being amused and maybe a little grossed out when the excited technician smeared brownish jelly all over Lisa's tummy. I wondered what we would see. I didn't expect to hear anything—but then remembered it's called an ultra*sound*. A swooshing sound began as the technician probed left and right—and then there she was, my daughter. "Do you see the head?" I said yes, but in all candor it was like deciphering a Rorschach inkblot—an apt image, as I would spend the next few decades wondering, "What is it?" The technician asked, "Do you see the heart?" I replied, "Not really." This tiny creature, who would change our lives and the lives of so many, was hiding in there, alive and pulsating, not big enough yet for Lisa to be showing.

How sad, and yet understandable, that life in utero has gotten politicized and has become the fulcrum that determines elections and Supreme Court appointments. Both the wee one within and the mother housing the wee one are medical marvels. Surely both merit rights and protections and attention and immense love. So much heart stuff is at stake: the fetus's minuscule heart beating just below and entirely because of the beating of the mother's far larger heart above.

No wonder *heart* is the word we use when we speak of love. When no one had ever met you, when the most visible you'd been was through that grainy ultrasound, you were loved; you were the cause of dreams, worry, and sometimes heartbreak. We think of newborns as dependent—and so they are. But if you want to see dependency, if you want an unrivaled portrayal of what grace and mercy are like, peer into the womb. Ponder that ultrasound snapshot or marvel at those startlingly beautiful photos somebody figured out how to take of intrauterine life. You were there. So was the person you love or the one who gets on your nerves. Tenderness and mercy must be required among us wonders of nature.

As if to ensure we'd have the most vivid image possible of what mercy is, God worked it out that the Hebrew language's word that we

translate "mercy" comes from the same root as the word for "womb."
Mercy is womb-like. We forever carry some dim recollection of how
warm and embracing that mercy was. You'll always crave a return
to that mercy.

You'll need that mercy, if you're a fetus or if you're a grownup
reading this book, for the journey ahead will be tougher than you
realize. Gorillas, baboons, and chimpanzees have it easier. Not only
do they not feel the anxieties that afflict us. Their birth is also more
straightforward, a direct shot out of their mother's womb. Human
infants have those twists and turns, the possibility of going breech.
Why are things so complicated for us? Is God still rankled about the
apple? "I will greatly increase your pangs in childbearing" (Gen. 3:16
NRSV). No matter how well obstetricians and midwives improve
their craft, childbirth is still extremely difficult and painful for the
mom—and for the equally helpless child inside.

Modern people scoff at the medieval notion that original sin is
transmitted to each person in the womb (with the possible excep-
tions of Jesus and his mother). Understandably, theologians tried to
reckon with the reality that every person inevitably and unfailingly
is a sinner—and right out of the womb. Whether or not you're fond
of the notion of original sin, you realize our immense need for God's
mercy—not merely once you're old enough to be accountable but
from birth, even from conception forward. And as we fully understand that all our human brokenness (whether it's baldness, allergies,
tendencies to depression or alcoholism, or mortality itself) is right
there at conception and in us always, we need not shrink back from
the idea that we most certainly are, as the hymn puts it, "weak and
wounded, sick and sore . . . bruised and mangled by the fall."[7]

Called from the Womb

If God is fully present in utero, if God somehow knit us together, if
God understands the complex realities of life in the womb and the
daunting challenges of the journey ahead better than we do, then
can we make sense of God's will, of God's desire for this fragile,
latent person in the making? Is God merely rooting for survival? If

mom and dad are already harboring dreams for this child, then how much more will God already be envisioning a holy, faithful life for this disciple-to-be? We think of God's calling as coming to attentive seekers, to young adults, or to those in midlife crisis. But in utero? Isaiah 49:5 teases out the idea that the prophet had been formed in the womb by God "to be his servant, to bring Jacob back to him" (NRSV). Jeremiah countered God's call by saying "I am only a boy" (NRSV); but then on further reflection, he began to intuit that God had actually been calling him even in his mother's womb (Jer. 1:4–10).

A fetus can detect sound at twenty-six weeks. Can it hear God? Does God call particular people, or all people, even in their mothers' wombs? What is calling anyhow? Is the divine call a voice out of nowhere? Isn't each person's sense of divine vocation a symphony of voices that call? Messages overheard from mom and dad, attributes and skills fostered in the womb and in later chance encounters, some church chatter and personal musings mixed in there: we process it all and infer that God is asking something of us. Frederick Buechner famously wrote that "the place God calls you to is the place where your deep gladness and the world's deep hunger meet."[8]

Fascinating: the world's deep hunger is out there, waiting for you to be born and notice; and your deep hunger is already there, festooned in your DNA, destined by the parents you happen to have and the place you'll happen to live. What if mom and dad begin, during pregnancy, to ponder that this unseen child is already being called by God? And what if you and I reminisce a bit and puzzle over what we probably missed back then—and since!—that God is calling us, even in utero?

To follow that calling, and frankly just to survive, mountains of help will be needed—from God and from others. God has wired us to need and to help one another, to be interdependent; the proof is in the way God made mother and child with two-way, not one-way, dependence. Unseen processes are happening not just to the child in utero but also to the mother—beyond her expanding belly and dizzying bouts of discomfort. Mark Sloan explains that there are hormonal surges "that prepare a mother's body for birth and breast-feeding," and that these surges "also bathe her brain, subtly altering her behavior in ways that prepare her to take on the role of mother."

Indeed, the nesting instinct is hormonal more than it is a learned behavior. These hormones flow from the fetus to the mother, as Sloan
describes it: "The little dictator in the womb is making sure that he
or she will be safe and healthy at birth, and that his mama will be
there for him until he's old enough to fend for himself."[9]

Quite beyond this involuntary preparation for life after birth, mom
and dad are out there nesting, studying, practicing, doing their best.
Mom avoids caffeine and alcohol and eats as well as she can manage,
allowing for nausea and occasional bizarre cravings. A conversation
is going on between mom and child about smell and taste: the child,
once out and growing up, tends to like the foods mom liked while
pregnant and tends to dislike the smells she abhorred.

Worship in Utero

Unable to stray from mom, the child experiences everything mom
does. The fetus hears and enjoys music, with bass tones penetrating
the fluid world of the womb better than treble. The sounds of mom's
speech, her breathing, the thump thump thump of her heartbeat,
the swirling of body fluids, dad's voice, siblings hollering, honk-
ing horns, and television all are muffled, soft, and indistinct to the
infant's ears. I wonder if parents who observe sabbath, some quiet
time of no stress or rushing around, might create a child with a taste
for peace and quiet, better equipped to "be still and know that I am
God" (Ps. 46:10).

After all, the child in the womb may already be a regular church
attender. I pause every time I come face to face with an expectant
mom in the communion line, and I am awed however briefly that I am
serving not one but two. This hidden one is already being nourished
by the body and blood of our Lord, who himself was nourished in his
mother's womb. Can the child inside hear my voice, even if muffled,
saying, "This is the body of Christ, the bread of life, given for you"?

The womb is dark, but not entirely. There is some color in there,
of lower wavelengths, violet, blue, dim, glowing. The human eye develops surprisingly early. There's not much to see yet, but just wait. If
you think you were just a little blob of nebulous tissue, you couldn't

be more mistaken: your eyes developed before your other body parts. Between the age of just three weeks (when mom doesn't know you exist yet!) and ten weeks (about the time you pose for your ultrasound), your optic vesicles, optic cups, corneas, lenses, retinas, and eyelids are formed. Want to ponder a miracle? A few ectodermic cells, directed by the master control gene called Pax-6, are transformed with dizzying rapidity into the organ of organs now fixed just beneath your forehead.

The complexity of the eye, even way back then, startles. Ask your optometrist to describe it all to you. And consider this: if in those earliest weeks in the womb, the curvature of the lens, the shape of the retina or the blood vessels in the stalks differed by just a few percentage points, you would see nothing or only vague, blurry blotches. The eyes you're using to read this book were fully crafted while you were in your mom. In that liquid, shadowy home, vague visual images were ticking into your brain receptors, beginning to soak up the wonders of creation you'd need dozens of lifetimes to absorb.

And your eyes were, in ratio to the rest of your body, almost comically huge, like the eyes of aliens in science fiction films. At fourteen weeks, in relation to the rest of your body, your eyes were four times as large as your eyes are now. A newborn's eye is two-thirds as big as it will ever be, while the rest of the body will grow twentyfold. The eyes in utero: outsized orbs, getting ready to see. Leonardo da Vinci, who painted the most penetrating, brilliant eyes ever placed on canvas, called the eye "the window to the soul."[10] And Jesus spoke of the eye as "the lamp of the body" (Matt. 6:22). The lids are closed—as if in prayer. Mary Oliver once asked,

> Do cats pray, while they sleep
> half-asleep in the sun?[11]

Do infants in utero pray? They might just be giving thanks for this miracle that arguably tops all others.

Jesus seemed hell-bent on people being able to see. He healed a man blind from birth, sparking ferocious rage from Jesus's foes (John 9). Jesus looked people in the eye, the eyes that God knit together in the womb, the windows to the soul that God had been looking into always. And when the blind were healed, the first person they saw was Jesus. A newborn today may see Jesus first too, in mom and dad, the people who are the designated members of Christ's Body to see and be seen.

Painful Squeezes

Finally, there is the discomfort and even pain undergone in utero. Pregnancy involves ever-escalating physical discomfort—for mom, of course, but for her child as well. It's tight in there, and the push out into the world is excruciating for the wee one and for mom. I'm a bit embarrassed to realize that I caused my mother intense pain for days and weeks prior to, and then during, childbirth. "I bruise you, you bruise me," as Art Garfunkel sang it—this hurting others and being hurt by them will persist, inevitably, through all of life.[12]

Think you've experienced some trauma, some tough situations? None probably match what you underwent in the hour of your birth. All that brutal mashing and shoving oddly saved your life. The violent spasms of the uterus not only push the baby out but also force the transfusion of blood from the placenta into the newborn.

With a playful imagination, Henri Nouwen pondered these pains that ferry us into life. In *Our Greatest Gift*, his thoughtful book about dying, he tells a story about fraternal twins talking with one another in the womb:

> The sister said to the brother, "I believe there is life after birth." Her brother protested vehemently, "No, no, this is all there is. This is a dark and cozy place, and we have nothing to do but cling to the cord that feeds us." The little girl insisted, "There must be something more than this dark place. There must be something else, a place with light, where there is freedom to move." Still she could not convince her twin brother.
>
> After some silence, the sister said hesitantly, "I have something else to say, and I'm afraid you won't like that either, but I think there is a Mother." Her brother became furious. "A Mother!" he shouted. "What are you talking about? I have never seen a mother, and neither have you. Who put that idea in your head? As I told you, this place

is all we have. Why do you always want more? This is not such a bad place, after all. We have all we need, so let's be content."

The sister was quite overwhelmed by her brother's response, and for a while didn't dare say anything more. But she couldn't let go of her thoughts, and since she had only her twin brother to speak to, she finally said, "Don't you feel those squeezes once in a while? They're quite unpleasant and sometimes even painful." "Yes," he answered, "What's so special about that?" "Well," the sister said, "I think that these squeezes are there to get us ready for another place, much more beautiful than this, where we will see our Mother face-to-face. Don't you think that's exciting?"

The brother didn't answer. He was fed up with the foolish talk of his sister and felt that the best thing would be simply to ignore her and hope that she would leave him alone.[13]

TWO

My Birthday

Comedian Gracie Allen used to quip, "When I was born, I was so surprised I didn't speak for a year and a half." Was your birth a surprise? Back in 1930, my father-in-law-to-be emerged from his mother's womb, and then everyone was flabbergasted when his twin brother followed a few minutes later. No one knew there were two. Many years ago, one of my church members called an ambulance due to horrific abdominal pain. A couple of hours later she delivered a baby boy she didn't know was in there.

My birthday? October 22, 1955. How many times have I written, typed, or spoken that trio of numbers, 10/22/55? Your identity is forever stamped with the date. And then each year you know it's a huge day, a day for a party or maybe somber regret or a wilting loneliness. John O'Donohue spoke of a birthday as an "echoing-day of your birth."[1] You were born. You're still here. Your coming to be, the reality of you echoes once more.

Are you fortunate enough to have cake, candles, and cards? How is your echoing-day marked? I have photos from childhood I can easily date by counting the candles. In one I'm wearing a fireman's hat. In another I'm sprawled across my sister's lap. I'm sure there was singing. The oldest, maybe corniest, and most repeated song in our lives: "Happy Birthday to You." Is it happy? If other days struggle to seem happy, is the birthday the exception? As a little girl, my sister-in-law, born on Flag Day, always felt special since total strangers apparently put flags out in celebration. Journalist and Christian activist Dorothy Day took her daughter, Tamar, out to plant radishes on her birthday each year.

You might shudder over the very real possibility of regretting the day you were born. Jeremiah did, and so did Job—not to mention Hector's wife, Andromache (in the *Iliad*), or Hamlet. Birth is an immense risk, more for the one being born than for anyone else. Who knows how things will turn out?

Hobbits, those wonderful, smallish creatures in J. R. R. Tolkien's Lord of the Rings series, mark their birthdays by throwing a party and giving gifts to others. When my children were young and obsessed with Lord of the Rings, they insisted that we do the same. Or rather, that I as dad do the same. And so it has been for decades now. On my birthday, my wife and children receive their hobbit birthday gifts from me. As it should be. I'm the grateful one who has been blessed.

Recalling Your Birth

Winston Churchill, who famously quipped, "All babies look like me; but then, I look like all babies,"[2] was asked quite a few times about his own birth. His parents, Randolph and Jennie, had only been married six months when Winston was born—yet they claimed he was premature, which no one believed. When asked about this, Churchill replied, "Although present on the occasion, I have no clear recollection of the events leading up to it."[3] Do you have any recollection of your birth? I was once asked this at a spiritual retreat. My knee-jerk response was, "Of course not." But then we do remember something. Maybe there's a photo or you've heard a story. Ask your mom, any mom really, to narrate the birth of her child, and she'll do it.

And no two stories are close to being alike. Each narrative is unique as a fingerprint, which tells us a lot about the peculiar delight God took in fashioning the universe to be a factory of ever new, unprecedented people like you and me. What if reproduction were cookie-cutter, mere breeding, an assembly line of one identical child after another, as if we woke up as characters in *The Handmaid's Tale*? Each person, even now that billions have been born through history, is unique.

Yet each peculiar person with a story is invited to become a part of the Body of Christ. Finding ourselves absorbed into that Body isn't the loss of our peculiar identity but the discovery of its fullness. C. S. Lewis helps us ponder this: "The Christian is called, not to individualism but to membership in the mystical body. . . . A row of identically dressed and identically trained soldiers set side by side . . . are not members of anything in the Pauline sense." He compares membership in Christ's Body to a family, the members of which "are not interchangeable. Each person is almost a species in himself. The mother is not simply a different person from the daughter, she is a different kind of person. . . . If you subtract any one member you have not simply reduced the family in number, you have inflicted an injury on its structure."[4]

So remember the day you were born, the day your long journey into the Body of Christ and eventually into the redeemed Kingdom of God commenced. There's much you cannot recall—and maybe some you wish you could forget. Adolf Hitler, as he rose to prominence, ordered all documents related to his birth to be confiscated. There may have been traces of Jewish blood! And his family had recently changed their name from Schicklgruber to Hitler. Can we imagine Nazis saluting with "Heil, Schicklgruber"?[5] More on the burdens we carry forward from birth later on.

The Miraculous Science of Birth

No one will narrate your birth story to you in this way, but the science of it is mind-boggling. One minute you're in the home you've known for months: aquatic, dark, cozy, squishy. Then the next minute you're out in the air, which you gasp to gulp in, breathing being something you've never attempted before. The oxygen, by nature's quirky design, floods your tiny system and signals to the lung's arteries and capillaries that it's time to relax, open up, and do new things.

Like crying. Usually crying is a clue that something's wrong. In the delivery room, the cry means, "Something's right" or "He's alive or "She's OK." The silence the newborn has kept for many months is broken. As an adolescent or grownup, you might dread silence or try to embrace it as a prayerful person once you get addicted to talking.

What an arduous transition your birth was and every birth is. The infant endures far more trauma than a grownup could bear. You've been mashed; your lumens are a mess; your pH has shifted dramatically. Somehow infants rarely go into shock. Wenda Trevathan points out that "such tolerance is not exhibited in adults who, if faced with the stresses that an infant experiences during parturition, would certainly experience shock and, likely, death."[6] It's bracing cold after the twenty-five-degree drop in temperature from inside mom to the delivery room. The bright lights make you squint. You're awfully sore from the pressure you've just endured.

You say goodbye to the placenta. Really you should frame it, this temporary, one-use-only organ that has sustained you—or maybe eat it, as many mammals and even some humans do. You're still attached to mom, whom you've still not seen, by a cord, which someone cuts. Good thing you can't reflect on this, as the severing of all that had nourished you all your life would scare the daylights out of you. Maybe once you're grown you'll learn that Walter Cronkite spoke of the flexible tube that moored spacewalker Ed White to his Gemini 4 capsule as an umbilical cord. Your cord gets cut; you're set adrift—although some invisible bond will keep you forever linked to the mother who bore you.

And still, as soon as one food source is cut off, another is provided. Once outside, the newborn discovers something about mom's body that is pretty different, and yet just as nourishing: the breast, toward which the newborn is lured innately and by God's created ordering of things. Mark Sloan explains, "One of the most amazing elements of the newborn's first-hour journey: a mother's nipple secretes a chemical that smells exactly like amniotic fluid."[7] How could this be? But then, how could it be otherwise?

You hesitate to describe a natural commonplace like childbirth, which has happened successfully countless times all over the globe, as "miraculous." And yet, even obstetricians with whom I've spoken get slack-jawed and marvel over the wonder of how you start as tiny cells being joined, growing, connected to a fleshy cord in a dark wet place, and finally emerging into an incredibly different environment. Carl Sandburg concocted these lovely words about a newborn:

> The finest of our precision watches, the most supercolossal of our supercargo planes, don't compare with a newborn baby in the number and ingenuity of coils and springs, in the flow and change of chemical solutions, in timing devices and interrelated parts that are irreplaceable. . . . Before man learned how to make an alphabet, how to make a wheel, how to make a fire, he knew how to make a baby.[8]

That you managed to be born is impressive, astounding, breathtaking, stupefying, wonderful, awe-inspiring. And your complex self has stuck around and actually works! You have good cause to wake up every morning, ponder your birth momentarily, shake your head, and move forward in wonder—and not get bent out of shape by so many little things.

Grading and Grace

You made your way out. Someone surveyed you to see if you were OK. Were you OK? Nerve-racking moments, the obligatory counting of fingers and toes. "Yes, she's breathing." "Oh my, he's squalling." When my firstborn, Sarah, was taken by C-section, they abruptly whisked her away to a far corner of the room, and some other nurses rushed in with considerable urgency, looking graver than I suspected was normal. Sarah had aspirated meconium, a serious but common enough event. Sometimes at birth, some heartbreaking reality is exposed. Sometimes immediate surgery is required. What's surprising, or downright unbelievable, is how many children actually turn out to be all right, given the odds of tiny cells multiplying exponentially inside a body and finally making the transition of all transitions from in the womb to out in the world.

But it's not merely whether you're OK. You get graded, right away, just as you'll get graded once you start school, in your working life, and even by people close to you throughout life. You'd think an infant wouldn't have such pressure right out of the chute. But in the 1950s, Virginia Apgar devised a score that still bears her name. A minute after birth, you get evaluated for your heart rate, respiration, reflexes, muscle tone, and skin coloration. Ten is a perfect score—and you can only imagine how many parents feel their competitive juices rising. "A perfect ten would be the perfect start for this excellent little one!" "Seven? We'll make up that deficit quickly I'm sure." "What do you mean, seven?" And then you're pricked for a quick blood test. Actually, with advances in technology, children are already getting evaluated in the womb!

Theologically speaking, this collides with what we want to say about the newborn—and those born decades ago too, before Virginia Apgar. It's not about test scores, high or low. It's all about grace. How did you do on your first test? Wherever you were from zero to ten, you were right then a wonder in God's eyes, the recipient of lavish grace, one who could never flunk so badly as to elude God's extravagant mercy.

You survived. You were "delivered"—a word worth lingering over. My grandfather delivered the mail. You get a pizza delivered. As a preacher I deliver sermons. As a teenager I delivered the morning newspaper. You must show up, rain, sleet, or snow. *Deliverance*, a novel by James Dickey, was made into a film (with an unforgettable banjo duet) by John Boorman that would make you shiver; only three of four urbanites survive sexual assault, ferocious rapids, and a stalker. And then we have the Bible, which speaks of Israel being delivered from Egypt and the Judeans being delivered from exile. The Psalms constantly ask for God's deliverance. God's habit of delivering culminated in Jesus (who'd been delivered by Mary) being delivered into the hands of those who finally crucified him (Matt. 20:18). Paul, exasperated by the law and his own inner inability to be holy, cried out, "Who will deliver me from this body of death?" (Rom. 7:24). At birth you are delivered; but the need to be delivered remains fixed in the plot of your life forever.

You cannot recall your delivery, which may be just as well. There was pain for your mother but also for you, being ruthlessly jammed through a narrow canal. At birth you were more malleable than you are now, but some newborns still suffer bruising and shoulder separations. This trauma provided fodder for Sigmund Freud, who deduced that the trauma of childbirth was the prototype of all trauma; the overwhelming stimulation of being born terrifies and imprints some horror onto the child's psyche, so then all later fearful experiences reduce you to that infantile state of helplessness.

Theology will forever clash with culture at this point. Society loathes helplessness. But Christian spirituality is all about realizing our helpless dependence, which isn't an embarrassing condition to be escaped but a holy truth to be embraced and lived into. The dependence of the newborn human being is more unusual than we realize. Mark Sloan points out that while human babies are born helpless, a newborn horse can run. A dolphin calf can swim immediately. Some monkey species actually assist in their own births: after being pushed a little way out, the infant monkey uses its hands and arms to push the rest of the way out. So American, these monkeys! Sloan sizes us up: "Our newborns require the most parental care, and for the longest period of time, of any mammalian species."[9] We think we're at the top of the food chain, the apogee of evolution, the crown of creation. But no, we are the weakest, the slowest. So humbling, as if God created things so we could learn and forever recall our primal dependence and how much mercy is required.

Tiny Evangelists

Yes, you begin in dependence, and you never shed that dependence. And yet, for the rest of your life, you want to do something, you want to matter, you want to make a difference. If you crave this sense that your life matters, then consider this: as soon as you were born, the world changed. And I don't mean the population of earth zoomed from seven and a half billion to seven and a half billion and one. Look around the birthing room. How much more impact will you ever have on anybody than you just had on your mother by being born? She will never be the same, even if she gives you up for adoption and never sees you again. If you stick around together over a few decades, you decisively and irrevocably change her, your dad, any siblings, your grandparents, and your family's circle of friends.

One impact you probably had when you were born was that you awakened something profound in your parents that even they never anticipated would be there. Dorothy Day wrote of the arrival of her daughter, Tamar: "No human creature could receive or contain so vast a flood of love and joy as I often felt after the birth of my child. With this came the need to worship, to adore."[10] You elicited unforeseen intensities of love, capacities for sacrifice no one knew they had in them. You may have functioned as a tiny evangelist, even if you've never evangelized anybody since. So many parents say, "I've never felt closer to God" or "God had seemed distant until my child was born."

All sorts of people were forever transmuted into somebody different when they were born. In *Anna Karenina*, Leo Tolstoy wonderfully narrates what unfolded for Levin while his young wife was in delivery. He leaped to his feet, rushed about, feared the worst, and demanded medical help when it seemed slow in coming. He lost all sense of time, and yet time stretched far beyond his wildest imagining. "There was nothing else to do but endure, every moment thinking that he had come to the ultimate limits of endurance and that at any moment his heart would burst." Trying to weather Kitty's ongoing shrieks, "he no longer had any desire for a child. . . . All he wanted was an end to this horrible suffering." But then it ended, that suffering, and she was safe—and the baby boy was safe. "The taut strings snapped. Sobs and tears of joy he had not in the least anticipated rose up within him with such force that they shook his whole body, and for a long time prevented him from speaking." Trying to grasp the shock, the wonder of this new life "seemed to him something excessive, a superabundance, and it took him a long time to get used to it."[11]

You had this sort of impact on someone and maybe on a couple of someones. Your first tangible, visible, and audible action was to inflict pain on the one closest to you—and you will continue to inflict pain on those you love for the rest of your life. In the thick of the pain, there also is joy. It's always light and shadow, pain and delight, fear and comfort, this life God gives us from birth. Maybe as you began to breathe, mom was being stitched up after surgery. Or maybe you were in crisis yourself, creating consternation where your parents had expected peace. The birthing room is like a microcosm of all that is to come, a narrow-angle lens through which the joys and sorrows of all of life are glimpsed.

My children made music minutes after they emerged from Lisa's womb. Without trying, they touched off the playing of Brahms's "Lullaby" all over Presbyterian Hospital. I am sure that random people strolling the hallway paused and smiled. And I am sure that others, in that moment of life and delight for us, were holding their bedside vigil over a loved one lingering near death. *Irony* isn't quite the right word. It's just how this life God designed for us is, and we dare not forget one or the other.

I've Just Seen a Face

Moments after you were born, you were seen. Oddly, your mother probably wasn't the first to see you. The doctor, nurse, midwife, and even your dad got to see you first. God created us for the peculiar interaction that is seeing and being seen. Eternal glory is described as seeing "face to face"—which is interwoven with "be[ing] fully understood" (1 Cor. 13:12). I will always wonder if people really see me; but then I tend to become whatever it is that people see in me. How I am seen, or even if I am seen, becomes the core narrative of my life.

The Beatles sang, "I've just seen a face I can't forget." Your face, which theologian David Ford calls "a distillation of time and memory,"[12] studied so carefully moments after your birth, will be the pivot of your relationships, that Janus-like demarcation between your inner and outer self. Your face will speak, smile, weep, kiss, eat, drink, sing, and pray. Your face will be admired or shunned. Your face will be photographed. Your face will grow, lose some of the baby fat, and finally succumb to weathering and wrinkling. Infants prefer faces to all other stimuli. A newborn prefers its mother's face to all other faces. We speak of facing our troubles or facing another day. What better blessing might there be for this new person than one that speaks of the face of God: "The LORD make his face to shine upon you" (Num. 6:25).

You were seen, and then you saw—for the very first time. Your eyes, Leonardo da Vinci's "windows to the soul,"[13] will be your windows to the world. And unless you wind up suffering vision trouble, those eyes will see so many amazing, beautiful, ugly, and pedestrian things. Your eyes will witness the pivotal and routine moments of your life. For now, at birth, you can't see well at all, maybe 20/400—which, as it turns out, is perfect. If you're a newborn, do you care what's happening outside the window or even across the room? You need to see mom, and she's right where you actually can see her.

What, really, is the first thing you see? You see selflessness. And you will never again see so much selflessness. You've just exited the haven of mercy, the womb—but all is well; there's more mercy out there. Mothers, having undergone physical trauma, and even surgery, never ask, "Am I OK?" but rather, "Is my baby OK?" Mom doesn't ask, "Does my hair look OK?" or "Are my clothes flattering?" but rather, "How does my baby look?" Lovely, isn't it?

The entire Christian ethic is exemplified in a mother's questions about her newborn—as Paul wrote, "Do nothing from selfishness or conceit, but in humility count others better than yourselves. Let each of you look not only to his own interests but also to the interests of others" (Phil. 2:3–4). When we approximate this, then we are of one mind with Christ, who somehow managed not to inquire about his own safety and security but gave himself entirely for others, for us. I wonder if Julian of Norwich pondered this when she spoke of Christ as "our true mother," a "kind, loving mother who knows and sees the need of her child [and who] guards it very tenderly."[14] Christ gives us life through his agonies, feeds us with himself, holds us close, and wants nothing more than for us to run to him, our true Mother, when we are in need.

What's in a Name?

Perhaps within moments, but sometimes after a day or two, your name, which you'll use, hear, say, write, and read a zillion times in your lifetime, is revealed. Some parents decide their child's name far in advance. I know one mom who, as each of her four children was born, looked the wee one over and declared, "Looks like a Stephen," and so he was, or "Looks like a Jennifer"—and so she was. Studies show that people, oddly enough, look like their names. Show an unfamiliar face to someone, and ask him to choose among three made-up names and the correct name; instead of guessing correctly the expected 25 percent of the time, people choose the right name nearly 40 percent of the time.[15] Most people, studies show, like their names—but others cringe, slightly, as I always did as a child when I heard my middle name, Comer.

For centuries, naming happened at baptism. I try to envision how very poignant it would be if we miraculously discovered video evidence of various responses to the priest's question, "What name is given to this child?" Hans and Margarethe Luther said, "Martin." Dorothy Day, a single mom, said, "Tamar Teresa" (as she was just then reading a book about Saint Teresa of Avila). The Hitlers said, "Adolf." Pietro and Pica Bernardone said, "Giovanni," not knowing people in Assisi would eventually call him by his nickname, "Francesco" or "Francis."

Lisa and I established some principles. We wanted biblical or theological names, names that had some currency in our family histories, names that would not easily admit of a nickname, and names that could never be misspelled. Three out of four of those worked for our eldest, as we flat-out forgot that sometimes people will leave the *h* off the end of Sarah. For number two, we had settled on Abigail—but after a long, arduous labor and a C-section, Lisa looked at me plaintively and asked, "Can we name her Grace?" I was in no position to argue. We went into labor and delivery for number three with mutually exclusive lists of possible girl names. Lucky for our marriage, Noah showed up.

What's in a name? In Bible times, parents didn't angle for cute or popular names. Each name was rich with meaning. Many single-word names are actually translatable sentences—and many have rich theological declarations. Micaiah (or Micah) means "who is like the Lord?" Mattaniah is "gift of the Lord." Ezekiel is "may God strengthen." Some names hint at tragic stories—like Ichabod, meaning "where is the glory?" (so dubbed for being born in a time when the people knew they were abandoned by God). Jonah means "silly dove"—and he was one. Caleb means "dog." Menachem means "comfort"—and you have to wonder if a child so named was regarded as a substitute for another child who'd been lost.

You have to pity the children of the prophets, as God often commanded the prophets to devise names that would be fiery sermons to the people. Did Isaiah's wife object or just shudder when Isaiah named one son Maher-Shalal-Hash-Baz, which means "the spoil speeds, the prey hastens," and then another Shear-Jashub, which means "a remnant shall return"? How did Gomer respond when Hosea named one son Jezreel, the location of Israel's bloodiest battle, and another Lo-Ruhamah, meaning "not pitied," and a third Lo-Ammi, "not my people"?

Your name is a sacred trust in God's heart, no matter who gave you that name. I love the way Scripture lets us overhear God speaking to people. God never said, "Hey, you down there!" God called each person by name—often repeating it, out of tenderness or to be sure the person actually heard. "Abraham, Abraham"—and Abraham would have preferred not to have heard what God said next (Gen. 22). "Samuel, Samuel" (1 Sam. 3). David echoed God's habit of this doubling when grieving the death of his son: "Absalom, Absalom" (2 Sam. 18:33). To the exiles, desolate and hopeless, God said, "I have called you by name" (Isa. 43:1). And what more powerful and tender theological thought has ever been expressed out of the heart of God than this? "I have graven you on the palms of my hands" (49:16). Your name is tattooed on God's hand. Ponder this for a few moments, and try to recall it for even a nanosecond every time somebody hollers your name or when you sign your name or when you state your name.

For various reasons, some people choose to change their name years after their parents anointed them with one. Maybe a married woman drops her middle name. Maybe you just never liked being Roscoe, so you go with Robert for the rest of your days. My favorite name change came on March 13, 2013, when Jorge Mario Bergoglio stunned the world by choosing to be known, after his election, as Pope Francis. Talk about pressure. His embrace of this name prompted biographers to say, "No one ever thought a pope could be called Francis; it would be like taking the name of Peter, or Jesus";[16] "the name Francis is a whole program of governance in miniature";[17] "it would have been a big contradiction for previous popes to choose the name Francis."[18] Like Saint Francis of Assisi, Pope Francis embraced as much humility and poverty as a pope could get away with. The day he was elected and assumed the name Francis, he even went back to the modest guesthouse to collect his things and pay his bill, explaining to the desk clerk, "I checked in under another name."[19] His mother, who at his birth had named him Jorge and dreamed he would become a doctor, would not have minded.

The Good News

How did word get out that you had been born? Phone calls may have been placed, or the doctor, nurse, or your dad staggered out to the waiting room where anxious relatives learned that you were you. Blue or pink balloons, a ribbon around the tree in your yard or on the mailbox, or one of those big wooden rental storks made the news more public, even to strangers passing by. In Kenya, midwives and other women huddle around the mother and begin a high-pitched, trilling, celebratory song called *nkimi*; four times for a boy, three for a girl, their thrilling chant wafting across the village.

Interestingly enough, when the news of your birth, or that of any child, is blurted out in the open, we experience a reiteration, the loveliest possible echo of what transpired when Jesus was born. Angels flew joyfully in the night sky and sang exuberant choruses announcing his birth—and God capped off the greatest birth announcement in history by placing a strikingly bright star in the sky above where Jesus lay. The Greek word for *gospel, euangelion*, means quite simply "good news." The arrival of life, for you, for one just met, for the ones you'll never know on the other side of the globe: the gospel quite literally in miniature. This is one more round of good news, and God is praised and joy abounds once more.

Remembering and ruminating on the day of your birth might serve as the bedrock of the spiritual life. You were never closer to God than you were in the moment of your birth. God, after all, came to be with us when Jesus was a newborn, like you, and with you. The Bible characterizes God as a laboring mother (Isa. 42:14), a nursing mother (49:15), and a midwife (Ps. 22:9–11). The joy your birth elicited is one with the joy of our resurrected Lord; at the Last Supper,

Jesus said, "When a woman is in travail she has sorrow . . . but when she is delivered of the child, she no longer remembers the anguish, for joy that a child is born into the world. So you have sorrow now, but I will see you again and your hearts will rejoice, and no one will take your joy from you" (John 16:21–22).

Remembering you did not will yourself into existence, that you were and are vulnerable, and that it's all about mercy and tender compassion: this is the infant's lovely reality and the persistent, ineradicable truth about your life at whatever age you are reading this book. How intimate, humbling, and glorious is the nature of this connection with God—as Annie Dillard describes it: "All day long I feel created."[20]

THREE

Unchosenness and Being Chosen

Before discussing Jesus, the greatest child ever, and why anyone would have a child, we'll pause here to let ourselves be dumbfounded by the sheer unchosenness of who we are moments after birth. We may well grow up in a culture that brags and gets passionate about freedom— but the balance of each person's life is pretty much determined and laughably predictable once we've sized up the basic facts immediately after birth.

And don't think for a moment that I mean that God has some sort of blueprint, a predetermined plan for each person. It's way less holy than all that, or it's a ridiculously different kind of holy. The religious question we'll have to wrestle with is this: Since so much is given, and granting that the basic plotline of a person's life is surprisingly unchosen, how do we make sense of anybody actually choosing God or being religious at all? And how does that fit with the Bible's obsession with people being chosen by God—to be part of the chosen people or simply recipients of God's gracious choice?

The Birth Certificate

Pick up any person's birth certificate and you'll have a pretty fair grasp on how that person's life will unfold. Mine bears my name, which I didn't choose, although I could change it I suppose. Then there's a date, 22 October 1955. That makes me a Libra—barely. Wish I'd been a Capricorn, like Jesus. Don't laugh: those astrologers found Jesus before the scholars poring over their Bibles figured it out.

In which month were you born? It matters. Malcolm Gladwell studied success in hockey and discovered that the vast majority of Canadian hockey stars were born in January, February, and March but precious few the rest of the year. Why? In Canada, the eligibility cutoff for age-class hockey is January 1. So when the seven-year-olds get into team hockey, those with January birthdays enjoy a huge advantage in physical maturity. And so they are chosen for special prep squads, where they get the best coaching and lots of adulation. Gladwell reveals similar effects in soccer, baseball, and even academics.[1]

When I started elementary school, the cutoff date was the end of October. So I was always the youngest in my class, shorter and not yet as agile as the far older kids. Later I would be the last to get a driver's license and the last to be able to purchase beer legally. Was I the lousy kickball player or the slow reader people thought I was? Or was I just 17 percent younger?

The year matters. I was born during the Cold War, McCarthyism, Ozzie and Harriet, and the advent of the civil rights movement. I baptized a child who was born the morning of 9/11. The song "Jumpin' Jack Flash" begins with an allusion to guitarist Keith Richards's birth in Dartford, Kent, bombed heavily during the Blitz: "I was born in a cross-fire hurricane." On the other side of the world, Carl Sandburg (in *Remembrance Rock*) told of an American baby born on "a day when the sky over Europe had never before been so full of bomber and fighter formations in death grapple."[2] The father was away fighting in the Pacific theater where, on August 6, 1945, the Enola Gay dropped a bomb nicknamed "Little Boy" (ironic, isn't it, given our topic?) on Hiroshima. Among the few survivors were mothers with children in utero, most of whom were born with microcephaly. In September 2015, a pregnant woman's home in Aleppo, Syria, was bombed. Her child, named Amel (meaning "hope"), was born with a shard of shrapnel lodged in her forehead. The mark of Cain.

Gender, Race, Place

Back in the day, when my children were born, the big surprise came when the obstetrician proclaimed, "It's a girl!" or "It's a boy!" Nowadays it's more likely an ultrasound technician who reveals on which side of this divide the fledgling person in utero will live. Gender, utterly unchosen, determines how people will size you up within a nanosecond of meeting you and how you feel inside your gut. People used to say my sister should have been a boy, as she could outhit, out-throw, and outrun any of the boys in the neighborhood. She never got that girls were made of "sugar and spice and everything nice." Ancient history? Stereotypes linger; they ossify. We have a tough, long slog ahead before we achieve genuine parity between genders in the workplace, in politics, and in church.

The body you're born with will fix what intimacy is like for you. Or will it? Whom will you love? Will you be the gender assigned to you on that birth certificate? Society is currently grappling with these issues. But hear Siddhartha Mukherjee's explanation: "It is now clear that genes are vastly more influential than virtually any other force in shaping sex identity and gender identity"— and so, "the capacity to reprogram gender using purely behavioral therapy and cultural reinforcement begins to tip into the realm of impossibility."[3]

Your race. How foolish of people to judge others because of their skin color. Who chooses to be white? Or black? My birth certificate says "white," and I have come to realize that I've always benefited from white privilege. We were poor when I was little, but nobody looked at me and thought "He'll never amount to anything" or "He's trouble." If you're born black in America, you have an increased likelihood of being pulled over by the police for no good reason or of causing the blood pressure of a fellow pedestrian to rise a little: all this is fixed at birth. Trevor Noah explains what growing up half-white and half-black in apartheid South Africa was like, how his very birth "violated any number of laws, statutes and regulations"[4]—hence the title of his witty and haunting autobiography, *Born a Crime*. He and his mom and his dad had to pretend they didn't know one another.

To glimpse the price of a secret life, the carnage experienced because of race, consider what Amos Oz wrote about growing up Jewish:

> The fear in every Jewish home, the fear that we never talked about but that we were intentionally injected with, like a poison, drop by drop, was the chilling fear that perhaps we really were not clean enough, that we really were too noisy and pushy. . . . A thousand times it was hammered into the head of every Jewish child that we must behave nicely and politely with the Gentiles even when they were rude or drunk. . . . We had to try very hard to make a good impression, because even a single child with dirty hair who spread lice could damage the reputation of the entire Jewish people. They could not stand us as it was, so heaven forbid we should give them more reasons not to stand us.[5]

Corroded dignity, undeserved, unchosen, inevitable.

Throughout your life, people ask, "Where are you from?" Whatever your answer, it's not a place of your own choosing. Shortly before William Shakespeare was born, his father John moved his family from Snitterfield to Stratford, "sparing posterity" (as Bill Bryson wittily put it) "having to think of his son as the Bard of Snitterfield."[6] We Americans might sing along with Bruce Springsteen's "Born in the USA," but most of us did not choose to arrive here. How could anyone be tempted toward national arrogance? The luck of birth? Am I luckier or more blessed than my friend Actionnel Fleurisma, who was born in Haiti? Jesus wasn't born in America but in an impoverished, backwater place in the Middle East that was subject to Roman tyranny.

In Charlotte, North Carolina, where I am writing this book, the single most accurate predictor of whether you'll go to college, earn a fair living, be healthy as an adult, or go to jail is the zip code your parents live in when you're born. Your zip code! Children's fates are fixed by something they won't know exists for several years. America boasts of its economic mobility—but it's rigid and harsh: where you're born and grow up defines you. Expand that to other continents. If you are born in sub-Saharan Africa, you'll most likely never live in a posh house, and your life expectancy is lowered. If you are born in Scarsdale, New York, you'll enjoy hair stylists, personal coaches, concierge medicine—and you'll have to go way out of your

way to get a glimpse at poverty. Mind you, other problems will afflict
you in such a place.

And, however humbling for readers of this book and for devout
people everywhere, the single most accurate predictor of whether
you'll be a person of faith as an adult is some mix of zip code and
your parents' churchgoing habits. Being born in the Bible Belt makes
you more likely to be a churchgoer than if you are plopped down in
Vermont or Oregon. Your parents won't likely take you to a Christian
church if you're born in Afghanistan. If your dad is a churchgoer,
you're more likely to become one than if only your mom attends. The
spiritual leanings of your birth family establish whether you'll grow
up with a fundamentalist or a liberal Protestant or a Catholic or a
Jewish or a Muslim worldview. People sometimes defy the circumstances of their birth and choose a different religion or worldview.
But not all that often.

Meet the Parents

The ultimate among the unchosens are your parents. These are the
people who will raise you, interact with you, nurture you, haul you
to the doctor and soccer practice, drive you crazy, love you in lovely
and then maddening ways, bless you, and unwittingly curse you.
Your political ideology, which you may feel very clever about, was
probably learned at a tender age at home—or else you are hell-bent
on not thinking what your parents thought. Either way, it's on them.

And you'll never be done with them. You may grow up and move to
another continent, but some invisible umbilical cord will forever tether
you to them. You will grieve their deaths, even if you weren't "close."
Maybe both your parents aren't in the picture. They divorced or one
died. Maybe both died and you were fostered or adopted. Maybe one
just deserted you. Talk about feeling unchosen. Or chosen.

Your pair of biological parents still have an immense, indelible impact on the person you become. Your genes (as we explored in chap. 1)
are some curious mishmash of their genes. My son is a dead ringer
for me; photos of him at age twenty-three are difficult to distinguish
from photos of me at age twenty-three. He also got my short legs

and embarrassing lack of a vertical leap. My daughters have their mother's (and her mother's) thyroid troubles.

Go for counseling and you'll wind up thrashing through parental stuff. When I do premarital counseling with couples, the simple inquiry, "Tell me about your parents and their marriage" (or even better, "What if your mother were married to his father?") elicits moans, laughter, the shaking of heads—and then I explain how these people, even if you don't see them much or if they're dead, dwell in your kitchen and bedroom once you've married. Was your family affectionate or reserved? When conflict popped up, did your parents stick their heads in the sand, or did they holler and throw things? The list goes on and on.

As if to underline how utterly unchosen these two most important people are, a chilling *Twilight Zone* episode envisioned a game show in which kids chose their parents from among vying contestants, including their biological parents (who inevitably lost). And there is a psychic haunting for most who are bedeviled in some way by unresolved parental "stuff"—which may explain why Jesus's best story was the one about the father who didn't behave like normal fathers and giddily embraced the dastardly son who'd squandered everything (Luke 15:11–32).

You didn't choose your parents' parents either. What's that old saying? "Jesus may be in your heart, but grandpa is in your bones." When one of my children first went in for counseling, the therapist started asking us questions, not about us as the parents but about our parents. I scoffed and said, "She hardly knows my parents." The therapist persisted. The Bible's seemingly prehistoric adages about trouble being visited to the third and fourth generations turn out to speak much truth. Depression, alcoholism, and other maladies find their way from grandparents to their children, sometimes skipping a generation. The genogram, that telling diagram of your family relations, highlighting brokenness and drama, can be a helpful tool in counseling and recovery—and another posterizing declaration that what matters in you is unchosen.

And the even longer genealogy, that long line of "begets," an obsession for many. How exotic to trace your ancestry to Charlemagne, Nefertiti, or Confucius! What a great scaffold to hang stories on!

Lisa's family tree features a signer of the Declaration of Independence. Mine, far fuzzier, has sharecroppers—and for some perverse reason I've longed to discover a long-lost horse thief or bank robber. Your genes have been snaking their way toward you forever.

My birth certificate was issued by the Department of *Health*. Immediately, at birth, patterns of your health, for life, are predictable: allergies, your rheumatological makeup, your proclivity toward various diseases. That's why they ask, "Is there a history of diabetes or cancer or heart trouble in your family?" We may strive to be healthy, to eat and exercise well, but there is a relatively narrow range within which we do so. Marathoners have heart attacks young. Smokers indulging in high-fat diets live into their nineties.

In *The Emperor of All Maladies*, Siddhartha Mukherjee's fascinating and ultimately humbling book about cancer and the surprisingly unsuccessful war we wage against it, tells the story of Hope and Prudence, identical twins who were offered a trial cancer screening in 1995. Hope said yes to the test. She had a breast tumor and underwent surgery and chemotherapy. She lived just five more years, dying in 2000. Prudence, suspicious of things medical, refused the screening. Four years later, in 1999, she felt a lump in her breast and then died on the same day as her sister Hope did.[7]

History can turn on such unchosen genetic matters. In 1904, the royal family of Russia, Nicholas and Alexandra, gave birth to a son, Alexei. The child bruised easily; his nosebleeds were hard to control. His mom turned to a legendary Russian monk (and a shyster as it turned out), Grigori Rasputin, whose influence infuriated an already angered proletariat. What no one understood was that Queen Victoria had a gene that caused hemophilia B, a lethal bleeding disorder, which she passed to her second daughter Alice, and then to Alexandra, the mother of Alexei.

Perhaps it's clear, and probably humbling to the nth degree when it comes to unchosenness, that the magical moment when your parents' genes found one another ultimately defines you. Mukherjee, in his later book, *The Gene*, simplifies things for us: "Gender. Sexual preference. Temperament. Personality. Impulsivity. Anxiety. Choice. One by one, the most mystical realms of human experience have become progressively encircled by genes. Aspects of behavior related largely or even exclusively to cultures, choices, and environments, or to the unique constructions of self and identity, have turned out to be surprisingly influenced by genes."⁸ Working out how God, grace, and faith are wedged into or enveloped around the hardwired determinism of your genes is a deft high-wire act.

The Thrownness of Existence

All this is obvious, once you think about it. The question is, How does all this unchosenness make you feel? Is it an immutable sentence you must fulfill or a delightful path to continue walking down? In America, the "land of the free," we feel free. But how free are we really? Aren't my choices dictated by the norms of the culture? What about my addictions—not merely to substances but to work or worry or diversions? How much of my life do I really choose? And how much of it, even as I feel like I'm flexing my free will, is at the heart of things unchosen?

The greatest minds of secular culture have discerned a kind of existential unchosenness about life in general. The philosopher Martin Heidegger analyzed all of us and spoke of the *Geworfenheit*, the "thrownness" of existence in this world, some banality, tinged with some dread.⁹ There is a stuckness of the soul. You just find yourself in the thick of the brute facts of the world, and the whence and why of your life are cloudy or blank—as if you woke up in a movie version of the book of Ecclesiastes.

And yet doesn't God give us free will? Even here, we realize our stuckness. Saint Augustine argued with Pelagius, just as Luther argued with Erasmus, about free will. The winning theological argument both times was and will always be that we might feel free, but we most certainly are not. We are shackled in our fallen, broken state. Sin is a choice—but then, not really. The inevitability of sin, the inescapability of the need for mercy, the crushing inexorability of our mortality: unchosen, and all the purest, most doggedly courageous choosing cannot elude our lostness.

When the Bible speaks of choosing, it's oddly not about us very often, stuck in unchosenness as we fallen creatures are. The Bible has very much to say, though, about God as one who chooses. God chose Israel. God chose David. God chose Christ. God chose the church. God chooses you and me. How can we make sense of being the chosen unchosen?

God Chooses Us

Here's what the Bible does reveal to all of us who are born into unchosenness: God is a God who chooses. How interesting to think of God—omniscient, omnipotent, omnipresent, ineffable, invisible, and unchangeable—as one who chooses. Such a God is personal and passionate and even countercultural. After surveying the lineup of Jesse's tall, muscular sons, God chooses the unlikely one, David, the small one, for the Lord does not see as we see (1 Sam. 16:7). Indeed, "God chose what is low and despised in the world, even things that are not" (1 Cor. 1:28). Want to see God's chosen people? Look through the hospital's nursery window at the array of infants lying in basinets, the ones with the birth certificates stamped with their unchosenness: there they are, God's chosen people. God chose you—at conception, at birth, and just as you were reading that last sentence.

I wonder if the author of 1 Peter had just spent time with a newborn, vulnerable, and beloved baby when he spoke of God's gracious choice: "You are a chosen race, a royal priesthood, a holy nation, God's own people, that you may declare the wonderful deeds of him who called you out of darkness into his marvelous light" (1 Pet. 2:9). The child is called from the darkness of the womb into the light of day. Somehow God's gracious choice of God's people is like that.

What it means to be the chosen people is beginning to emerge. Why did God choose Israel as God's chosen people? Deuteronomy 7:7–8 explains why: "It was not because you were more in number than any other people that the LORD set his love upon you and chose you. . . . It is because the LORD loves you."[10] Why does God choose Israel? It is because God loves Israel.

We call this sort of divine love "grace." Grace embraces the unchosen. Grace is itself unchosen. That you will live into this grace is God's plan for your life. But be careful here: grace is the antithesis of

modern, pet notions about "God's will" or "God's plan for my life."
You grow up in Texas, marry a Baptist, and land a partnership in a
law firm—and that's "God's plan for your life"? This widely held
notion has zero basis in Scripture, and it demeans the loving heart
and holiness of God. Followed to its logical conclusion, this picture
of "God's will" leads us to imagine God condemning a newborn to be
born into an abusive home, or a new mom to go home to a husband
who beats her. God has dreams for us, but the heart of God is so loving that it would recoil from any hint of determinism. Wise parents
don't cram their children into expectations and a schedule fixed at
birth; how much less would God our blessed Father do such a thing?

Grace is the answer to the riddle of how the life of faith happens
in a life largely unchosen. You are who you are—and the struggle to
fix, improve, or even deny who you are is resolved by grace. I know I
was personally transfixed and virtually reconverted when I first read
Paul Tillich's unforgettable sermon, "You Are Accepted."[11] I wonder
if he had a newborn infant in mind when he spoke so beautifully of
the moment when "a wave of light breaks into our darkness" and
we hear God's voice saying, "You are accepted. You are accepted,
accepted by that which is greater than you. . . . Do not try to do anything now; perhaps later you will do much. . . . Simply accept the fact
that you are accepted! If that happens to us, we experience grace.
After such an experience we may not be better than before, and we
may not believe more than before. But everything is transformed. . . .
Grace transforms fate into a meaningful destiny; it changes guilt into
confidence and courage." Grace? Acceptance? These are not inscribed
on the birth certificate—but they are implied and championed on
the baptismal certificate. Confidence? Courage? Not on the birth
certificate either—but much will be required.

Choosing beyond Our Chosenness

Grace came to Israel—that is, Israel was chosen by God—not to
bask in God's exclusive attention but for a huge task, for a worldwide
purpose. God chooses Israel; God chooses the church; God chooses
any- and everybody to be God's ambassadors (2 Cor. 5:20). Jesus

chose his disciples "out of the world" (John 15:19) to be sent into the world. God chose Abraham and his descendants so they might be God's blessing to everybody else (Gen. 12:1–4), to be a "light to the nations" (Isa. 49:6), to "go into all the world" (Mark 16:15), to "be my witnesses" (Acts 1:8). God's people are chosen for this mission: to reveal to all the other people that they too are chosen. Walter Brueggemann coined a memorable phrase as a corrective to any sense of arrogance or entitlement: "The chosen must choose beyond their chosenness."[12]

This is hard for us genetically programmed creatures. Richard Dawkins tells the truth about even the noblest of us who are the manifestation of our genes: "We are survival machines—robot vehicles blindly programmed to preserve the selfish molecules known as genes."[13] You may wish to be broad-minded and altruistic. But, "be warned that if you wish . . . to build a society in which individuals cooperate generously and unselfishly toward a common good, you can expect little help from biological nature. . . . We are born selfish. Let us understand what our own selfish genes are up to, because we may then at least have the chance to upset their designs."[14]

Newborns are utterly and even charmingly selfish. Maturity dawns when we can push selfishness aside. For those reading a book with a theological slant, the dream is that the remedy to our selfishness, the disruption of our genetic inevitability at birth, will be the church, the life of faith, God's saving intervention. You choose beyond yourself only when empowered by God's Holy Spirit. You surprise yourself with some holy act, contrary to your selfish nature—leading you to exclaim, "It is no longer I who live, but Christ who lives in me" (Gal. 2:20).

We can see how God's choosing overlaps with God's calling. When God calls someone, that person's credentials and ability to get the job done are on par with the résumé a newborn infant might offer. Moses cannot speak; Jeremiah is too young; Isaiah isn't holy enough; Mary has never been with a man. Jesus's disciples were chosen, but Jesus didn't do any background checks; they were just standing around by the water's edge.

This un-American notion that it's not about qualifications, experience, or hard work is humbling—and then liberating. Sadly, God's people indulge in the bad habit of twisting God's calling to vaunt their made-up superiority. But God's way is exemplified any time we see any child anywhere being born. Only then can everyone's unchosenness, and then chosenness in God's eyes, be embraced. Rabbi Jonathan Sacks, pondering what it means for the Jews to be God's chosen people, says, "God, the creator of humanity, having made a covenant with all humanity, then turns to one people and commands it to be different, teaching humanity to make space for difference."[15] And then we find God in difference.

And we find work to do in the unchosenness of others. Back in 2004, migrant workers Abraham Candelario and Francisca Herrera gave birth to Carlos, who was born with an extremely rare condition called Tetra-amelia syndrome, which meant that he did not have arms or legs. Nearby, six weeks later, Jesus Navarrete was born to Sostenes Maceda, with a severely deformed jaw. Two days later, Maria Meza bore a child with one ear, no nose, one kidney, and no sex organs; the child died after three days. The culprit? Thalidomide, deployed by their employer, Ag-Mart Produce.[16] What do unchosen choosers do to ensure such injustice never happens again? When children suffer unchosen injustice, they are the direct voice of God calling on God's people to get angry and not rest until something changes.

We, the chosen unchosen ones, have this justice work to do and some interpersonal work too. We extend grace everywhere. Robert Plomin, after explaining (in *Blueprint: How DNA Makes Us Who We Are*) how genetics determines everything, including psychological states we usually attribute to parenting or experience, suggests that we therefore have good cause to be tolerant and even merciful toward others—and ourselves.[17] If people tend to be overweight or don't like school or are hard to love or are maddeningly impetuous, genetics is the reason, and ours is to understand and be gentle.

We began by saying that all the important, identifying facts of your life are set at birth and are quite unchosen. And then we are surprised by the delightful fact of being chosen, even before birth, by God to be God's own and to be given the most meaningful life purpose imaginable. The truth and reality of this is rooted in God's choice of his own infant son, Jesus, who was born to be one with us. Joined forever to him in our birth, our future is settled in advance. To how God chose us in the birth of Jesus, we now turn.

PART 2

JESUS'S BIRTH AND EARLY LIFE

FOUR

Mary, Mother of Our Lord

If we want to make theological sense of our own birth, if we want to begin to understand God's intimate connection with us as far back as conception, we can do no better than to ponder the marvelous story of Mary, the mother of our Lord. "Ponder" is just what she, understandably, did after those mystical and perilous nine months from the first stirrings in her womb to the arrival of her son, God's son. As she tried to rest, exhausted and yet jubilant after delivering the most wanted, unexpected, and desperately needed child in all of history, "Mary kept all these things, pondering them in her heart" (Luke 2:19).

She "kept." Luke's Greek word implies "treasuring." And which of "all these things" did Luke have in mind? I suspect that she treasured more than just the shepherd's crazed report of an angelic choir, the agony of birth, the months of uncertainty during her pregnancy, the arduous journey to visit Elizabeth, Joseph's tender mercy, or even Gabriel's unasked-for visit. Wouldn't she have treasured the simplicity of her old life in Nazareth? Was it hard to treasure her interrupted dreams—not to mention what Rowan Williams called "the dangerous difference that God's Word would make"?[1]

All these things she "pondered"—the English word is derived from the Latin *pondus*, meaning "weighty." We ponder what is substantial, maybe a burden; to ponder what is heavy, strength is required. The Greek suggests something even more picturesque behind "pondered": *symballousa*, meaning literally "tossing around together" or "debating." Have you ever had so much substantive stuff in you at once that it seemed to churn incessantly? Batting it around with yourself, you almost can't help opening yourself to God. Richard Rohr sees Mary "in that liminal space between fascination and attraction on the one side, and fear and awe on the other."[2]

Luke tells us that Mary "pondered" again when twelve-year-old Jesus got lost (but not really lost) in the temple (Luke 2:51). We can be sure she pondered much as Jesus grew up, left home, gathered a passionate following, and then clashed with the authorities. We shudder over what she must have pondered on that dark night after his crucifixion. And in the long years to come after his resurrection and ascension, who pondered (and missed) him more than Mary?

Cause for Wonder

Luke's telling observation of how Mary treasured and pondered all these things invites us to do the same, gifting us with considerable liberty to do so creatively. Mary: What woman's name has been repeated more times in human history? Who has been the subject of more paintings, statues, jewelry, and carvings? How many have fingered rosary beads, mindlessly or in desperation?

Theologians have argued over her so vehemently that violence has broken out. Was she to be dubbed *theotokos*, "God-bearer"? Was she immaculately conceived? Perpetually virgin? Assumed bodily into heaven? Heated debate usually grows in the soil of deep passion, and the church's passion for Mary has moved her devotees to devise eloquent words and music about her—like this, from Saint Ephrem the Syrian way back in the fourth century:

> Your mother is a cause for wonder: the Lord entered her
> and became a servant; He who is the Word entered
> —and became silent within her; thunder entered her
> —and made no sound; there entered the Shepherd of all,
> and in her He became the Lamb, bleating as He came forth.[3]

Or this, from Rowan Williams: "How can anyone carry God, bring God to birth in the world? How can you carry the cup without spilling it? But what if the cup is no fragile container but a deep well that can never run dry?"[4]

In the famed aria "Ave Maria," we hear the angel Gabriel's perspective on Mary. In Amy Grant's song "Breath of Heaven," Mary expresses fear and doubts her own wisdom. She questions whether the Lord should have chosen another for his mother and begs him for help and strength, acknowledging that only the "breath of heaven" can hold her together. Matt Lowry, Kenny Rogers, Kathy Mattea, CeeLo Green, Reba McEntire, Rascal Flatts, and a host of others have recorded "Mary Did You Know?" No matter what Gabriel had said, how could Mary conceivably have known that Jesus would walk on water, calm the storm, and one day rule the nations?

This heaping of attention on Mary would make her blush, and she would gently insist that we stop. Martin Luther was right: "Mary does not desire to be an idol; she does nothing, God does all."[5] Her loveliness, her holiness, and her appeal reside in her unawareness. A simple young woman saying yes to the life of God already growing in her: without realizing it, she was now the Ark of the Covenant, the Holy of Holies, the open space where the infinite, uncontainable God became finite, contained in her womb.

An Illiterate Reader of the Word

So much we've spoken of here is the result of imagination and pondering—so skeptics will argue that we cannot know such things. Here's what we do know. Mary lived in Nazareth, a small, backwater village of no account, population in the dozens, her family and neighbors eking out a hardscrabble existence. We would say that she married young—but so did most women back then. Even cynics will grant that she had a son, probably other children, and a husband, Joseph, who was a carpenter or stone mason.

We yearn to see her face. Much of Christian art depicting her is kitschy. I have always been fond of the serene, lovely paintings of her by Giovanni Sassoferrato—although her skin is terribly white, while

FIGURE 2. *Mother and Child*, c. 1906 (oil on canvas), by Garibaldi Melchers (1860–1932)

the real Mary would have been, like Middle Easterners of her race and place, more darkly complected. To visualize the feel of Mary's face, we might veer toward something like Dorothea Lange's iconic *Migrant Mother*, a 1936 photograph of a mother exhausted and yet courageous. Herbert O'Driscoll's wise devotional book about Mary, *Portrait of a Woman*, features Garibaldi Melchers's *Mother and Child* on the cover (see fig. 2). This mother's more weathered complexion suggests strength and gentleness; her expression suggests she's endangered and exhibits a ferocious kind of love as she shields her child from danger.

We are pretty sure Mary was illiterate. Certainly as a poor young woman from the middle of nowhere, she didn't own a book; her family didn't have their own Scripture scrolls. But she would have seen the scrolls unfurled in the synagogue and listened attentively to the regular readings. Like most devout Jews, she would have committed the Psalms and much more of the Old Testament to memory. She and her son were Israelites, the people of God's promises. Thomas Torrance puts it elegantly: "And then at last in the fullness of time, when God had prepared in the heart and soul of Israel a womb for the birth of Jesus, a cradle for the child of Bethlehem, the savior of the world was born, the very Son of God."[6]

Through the centuries, artists have tried to figure out how to paint or sculpt that shimmering moment when the angel came to Mary and asked her to let Jesus take on flesh in her. Almost always, as the artists have reckoned it, she is holding an open book: God's Word. The angel didn't enter her life in a vacuum. Mary was a student of God's Word; when asked to become the mother of God, she replied, "Let it be to me according to your Word" (Luke 1:38).

Martin Luther called Scripture "the swaddling clothes in which Jesus is laid." To ponder Mary's pregnancy, we ponder the Scriptures that were very much alive in her mind and heart during those days of anticipation, anxiety, discomfort, and probably nausea, while something was going on inside her that she could not entirely fathom. Her pregnancy was unique, and yet she was like all mothers in waiting. The Psalms resonated, with their dark cries for help and comfort. I wonder if she was deeply moved to reconsider the story of Hannah, barren and then surprised with a son? Once Samuel, Hannah's dream, her lovely gift from God arrived, she didn't cling to him but gave him back to the Lord, to serve with Eli in the temple at Shiloh. That boy in turn heard a voice in the night, and after some confusion responded, "Speak, LORD, for your servant is listening" (1 Sam. 3:9 NRSV). Did that moment shape her reply to Gabriel, "Let it be to me according to your Word"?

Which texts spoke most deeply to her? Did she have favorites? Surely the stories of Hannah's pregnancy and the stirrings in Rebekah's womb moved her. The blessing in Numbers 6:25 ("The LORD make his face to shine upon you, and be gracious to you") must have resonated encouragingly. When the birth pangs were intense, did her mind drift to Psalm 22:1, "My God, my God, why have you forsaken me?" (NRSV), as her son's did in his hour of agony? After he was gone, what pulsated in her heart when she heard 1 Corinthians 13:7 ("Love bears all things, believes all things, hopes all things, endures all things"), which could have been circulated and read where she lived out her years? What if pregnant women or young mothers read Scripture during their days of wonder and struggle, picturing Mary pondering the words in her heart?

When Jesus was grown, he would reflect on Scripture, frequently adding, "He who has ears to hear, let him hear." Hadn't he been moved by his mother's attentive ear? Pre-modern people, lacking books, science, and cynicism, had a far higher expectation of the immanence of the holy. Their world was more "enchanted" (C. S. Lewis), "porous" (Charles Taylor), or at least "semipermeable" (James Kugel).[7] How advanced was Mary along this spectrum of the intensive, naive, vulnerable, or expectant? John of Damascus, an eighth-century Syrian monk, taught that Mary conceived through her ear. Saint Ephrem, the fourth-century mystic also from Syria, penned these elegant words:

> Just as from the small womb of Eve's ear
> Death entered in and was poured out,
> so through a new ear, that was Mary's,
> Life entered and was poured out.[8]

The Echo of Her Calling

Mary perceived the new life dawning in her belly as a call, as her divinely ordained vocation. Having a child wasn't her pursuing fulfillment or seeking security in old age. She was responding to God's calling. Or we could say the nascent life in her became her calling. When the news sinks in that, yes, they are pregnant, how do mothers begin to discern, like Mary, what God is asking of them and how nurturing their child in the womb and after birth can embody a life of service to God, a determination to follow the One whom Mary nurtured in her womb?

Tradition suggests that Mary was about to draw water from a well when she was interrupted by the angel. A well in Nazareth supposedly marks the place, housed in a massive basilica that fields more visitors every day than the entire population of the Nazareth Mary knew. There is something mystical about water, our thirst for it, the beauty, the shimmering ripples that elicit simple awe. Water will matter for her and for all mothers. They need to stay hydrated. Their fetuses live in a numinous, aquatic realm until the water breaks. And then a lifetime of taking baths and drinking water, baptism, and delight in rivers, lakes, ocean waves, and gentle rains.

The appearance of the angel must have been terrifying. Gabriel was, in Jewish lore, a mighty warrior among God's heavenly host. And yet, if God's plan was to make God's mind and heart accessible, and for people not to be terrified, perhaps Gabriel toned it down or came in a more humble guise. Luther suggests that "Gabriel did not resent being used as an errand boy to carry word to a lowly maiden. His glory was laid aside, and he appeared to her simply in the guise of a comely youth."[9] Even if he showed up in the most inviting form imaginable, Mary still had good cause to shiver. Elie Wiesel was right: "If an angel ever says, 'Be not afraid,' you'd better watch out: a big assignment is on the way."[10]

Isn't our assignment similar? Herbert O'Driscoll captured our inevitable kinship with Mary:

> She had felt the divine visitation which in some way comes to us all. What had been asked of her was unique, and yet an echo of it reaches all of us if only we have ears to hear. She had been asked to offer herself to the divine will, to become a servant. She had made her choice, as we all must. Fully and freely she had said Yes. For those who say Yes nothing is ever the same again.[11]

God's calling to us is always like it was to Mary: God asks to become real in us, to take on flesh in our lives.

In the Bible, those who are called have their reasons not to say yes. Moses has his speech issues; Jeremiah is too young; Isaiah is unholy—and now Mary, who knows their stories, has not been with any man. God always counters and uses the unusable. We might ask, "Why Mary, of all people?" We presume she was of immense holiness; Wordsworth called her "our tainted nature's solitary boast."[12] She calls to us out of her holiness; Richard Rohr suggests that "somehow she is calling all of us to our absolute best."[13] She was a virgin. But in those days, as a matter of both holiness and family honor, most newly betrothed women were—hence, not the shock this would be today. Luther pinpoints her humility—a humility that did not even know it was being humble: "She gloried neither in her virginity nor in her humility, but solely in God's gracious regard. . . . True humility does not know that it is humble."[14]

Her ordinariness, and in such an ordinary place, makes her the sort of person God would choose for this extraordinary mission. Ultimately, what we realize about Mary is not that she has this or that ability; what she has is simply availability. "Let it be to me," she says. As with all of us, God is looking for readiness, availability, or what Maggie Ross calls "a willingness for whatever."[15] Mary hears the angel speak of what is impossible. With considerable courage, naivete, and trust, she goes with it; she lets it be in her. And I feel sure that over time she came to realize what was dawning in her was not only for her or even her people but also for the whole world.

When people think about being born, and when they fix their attention on Mary, they eventually begin to realize the wisdom of Meister Eckhart, the fourteenth-century German mystic:

> We are all meant to be mothers of God. What good is it to me if this eternal birth of the divine Son takes place unceasingly but does not take place within myself? And what good is it to me if Mary is full of grace if I am not also full of grace? What good is it to me for the Creator to give birth to his Son if I also do not give birth to him in my time and my culture? This, then, is the fullness of time. When the Son of God is begotten in us.[16]

Joseph the Merciful

Mary had a fiancé, which is way too fancy and romantic a word. There were no wedding planners, photo shoots, or engraved invitations.

They simply were betrothed, committed to marriage. Without picturing anything overly romantic, we can be sure Mary cared deeply for Joseph—especially after his gracious dealings with her. Matthew 1:19 portrays Joseph as "righteous" (NRSV). Was he a titan of holiness? We know he was also something humbler and more difficult: he was merciful. We can only guess at the terrible swirl of emotion he felt, perhaps anger or even revulsion, when she told him what was unfolding. Surely he overheard whispers around town and was targeted with chilly stares. But somehow, after hearing from the angel, he didn't jettison her or the impending marriage. He remained still and constant. He was quiet and prayerful enough to jibe with God's Spirit. He stayed. He was merciful.

Probably he had been shown mercy himself and understood the need for it. This construction worker, who labored hard for a living, no doubt continued to be a merciful father to this child that was his, but not entirely. Our children are ours, but not completely. Mercy is required. Was there any of Joseph's mercy in Jesus's mind when, as a grownup, he said, "Blessed are the merciful, for they shall obtain mercy" (Matt. 5:7)? Or when he told the story about a father who was merciful to his prodigal son (Luke 15:11–32)?

Every Christmas pageant has a Joseph, but he never gets a speaking part. He just stands, gazing, holding the donkey's reins. No acting skill required. He's just there. There are unrecognized characters in all our stories—the seemingly inconsequential people who just show up, who are there, who are steady, who seek no attention for themselves. Mary was the lucky one, truly "blessed among women."

Every mother dreams of, and often is blessed with, a Joseph (or two or three): someone who simply shows up and stays, watchful and caring, solid and consistent; someone who offers a ministry of presence, the humble marvel of simply being with another person. Jesus was a lot of things, but mostly he was God with us, Immanuel. Like Joseph.

The Visitation to Elizabeth

What did Mary do to keep busy during the months she was with child? Luther spoke of the ordinariness of her days: "She behaves just as she did before any of this was hers—seeks no greater honor, is not puffed up, vaunts not herself, calls out to no one that she is the mother of God, but goes into the house and acts just as before—milks cows, cooks, scrubs the kettles, and sweeps the house like any house."[17]

She also packs her things and goes on a long journey to Ein Kerem, just west of Jerusalem, to visit her relative Elizabeth, who was way past childbearing age and yet pregnant herself. In Ein Kerem today a couple of elegant churches, featuring paintings and statues of these two women embracing, mark the spot. It would be hard to imagine a more lovely, poignant meeting than that between these two holy women. Both were staggered by the news of their impossible pregnancies. Both were likely uncomfortable, fearful of death in childbirth, and worried for their vulnerable child's survival. Mary, responsible for safely bearing God's son, took a risky journey. Almost a hundred miles, rugged roads, steep ascents and descents. She was hungry for good company. We could say, as Richard Rohr puts it, she became "the first missionary to take Christ out into the world."[18]

Ponder the moment: Mary entered the room, and she spoke, probably using the usual greeting, "Shalom!" Peace. Ah, the child in her womb would be the Prince of Peace! Then Elizabeth, overjoyed to see her, felt an unusually strong kick in her side. Infants in utero can hear, although voices are muffled. John apparently heard her, and almost magically managed to perceive his little cousin in the other woman's womb, and with uncommon pre-birth genius he understood the greatness of the other boy—and this caused him to leap, a spasm of recognition and giddy delight. John would always, until his life was cut short by Herod's jealous violence, be deferring to Jesus, pointing to the one trailing a ways behind him, especially down by the bank of the Jordan River. Karl Barth adored Matthias Grünewald's painting of Christ's crucifixion, which depicts John the Baptist standing near the cross, pointing a crooked finger in Jesus's direction; Barth dreamed of being like John's pointing finger, as we all might.

We all need someone to point the way for us. With much insight, Jeremy Troxler envisions Elizabeth as a mentor to Mary. The sorrows Elizabeth had endured wrought in her considerable wisdom. Like all mentors, Elizabeth was simply there, ready, available, and receptive. She listened. And her few words were the right words, helping Mary to remember that it's all about God. "Her mentor's joyful welcome and sensitivity of soul create a safe and sacred space where Mary can sing her own song of praise for who she is and for what God is doing in her life."[19]

We need good company as we move toward any new life, especially the birth of a child; what greater gift can God give? Elizabeth and Mary's most pregnant of all conversations proved to be unforgettable. Elizabeth's insight, "Blessed are you among women," has been repeated billions of times in every place on earth and in countless languages as part of the recital of the Rosary (Luke 1:42). And then Mary, of all things, sang (vv. 47–55). Her song is theologically vibrant and culturally revolutionary. But I try to listen just for her voice. Surely she wasn't one of those powerful sopranos with a ton of vibrato. I picture a gentler, clearer voice, singing when she might have merely spoken—like lovers in the movies do. "He who sings prays twice," Saint Augustine is supposed to have said. She must have sung at other times during her pregnancy; Jesus in utero surely overheard. And then when he was born, she had to have sung to him often. Did he recall her intoning Psalm 22 or 30 to him as a child when he uttered those prayers as he hung on the cross? Did she, as she watched in horror?

She had come to Elizabeth "with haste" (Luke 1:39)—anticipating the way the grown Jesus did whatever he did "immediately" (a word used eleven times just in Mark chap. 1). Maybe she hustled home to Nazareth. Did she feel any pre-contractions along the way? She would have been wise to have trekked directly to Bethlehem from Ein Kerem, a mere eight miles away. If we believe the Bible's itinerary though (some do, while others wonder if it's symbolic), after the hundred mile trip home to Nazareth, she turned around and journeyed another hundred miles south to Bethlehem with Joseph.

Her labor commenced—back in the day when at best you had a midwife trained only by trial and error, no spinal blocks, no medications, no labor and delivery room. Sanitation was questionable, although they didn't know this. Every young woman had heard the screams of relatives and neighbors in childbirth. Every woman had grieved friends and relatives who had died trying to bring their babies into the world or whose children had died in the process. The terror for Mary, even if she had thought she'd heard an angel months earlier, made her shiver.

Was her labor long or short? We might wish that God, in God's unfathomable mercy and special care for this mother, spared her the worst agonies—although if the rest of the story gives us any clues, when God's plans for this child involved political harassment, arrest, whipping, and the horrors of crucifixion, we might wonder if Mary's labor was the hardest there has ever been.

Saint Augustine, enraptured by Mary, wrote, "In conceiving you were all pure, in giving birth you were without pain."[20] He should have consulted Monica, his own mother, on this. Rachel Marie Stone fills in the blanks of the biblical story more fittingly:

> *A girl was in labor with God.* She groaned and sweated and arched her back, crying out for her deliverance and finally delivering God, God's head pressing on her cervix, emerging from her vagina, perhaps tearing her flesh a little; God the Son, her Son, covered in vernix and blood, the infant God's first breath the close air of crowded quarters. . . . God the Son, her Son, pressed to her bare breast. . . . God the Son, her Son, drank deeply from his mother. *Drink, my beloved. This is my body, broken for you.*[21]

After enduring much pain and outright terror, and with so little assistance, "she gave birth to her first-born son and wrapped him in swaddling cloths, and laid him in a manger" (Luke 2:7). Onlookers did what they could, but they must have shuddered over the loss of blood, with no antibiotics or pain relievers, no suctioning of the infant's lungs, no physician within a hundred miles. They must have held their breath during those agonizing seconds before Jesus's first cry. Mary held him to her breast, voiced a prayer of gratitude. She nursed him, toyed with his fingers, sang to him, and rocked him, beaming with pride when onlookers gazed into that tightly knit realm of tender love.

And there it is. The reason for all of creation, the beauty that is God, the epitome of truth, the love we've known and craved and tried to give, our very destiny: all right there in that embrace of mother and child. Peek over Mary's shoulder, or over any new mother's shoulder, as she caresses her child. Maybe you've been in that most beautiful curled-up circle yourself. But of course, you have been! You were once that small, that vulnerable and needy. Someone held you, and you've never been closer to God than in that moment. A mother's cradling of new life is the clearest possible window into God's heart.

Who cut the umbilical cord between Jesus and Mary? A young woman who happened by the stable, trying to be helpful? Joseph? Though the umbilical cord may be cut, the deep bond of mother and child is unseverable. Or is it? There will be loss; this cutting anticipates more to come for Mary. But for that pristine moment of birth: when the light of the world had dawned inside Mary's body and then was enveloped in her arms, we finally see our true selves and the true God-with-us in the glow. I admire an Ethiopian prayer to Mary from the ninth century that doesn't overstate things at all:

> Your hands touched him who is untouchable and the divine fire within him. Your fingers are like the incandescent tongs with which the prophet received the coal of the heavenly offering. You are the basket bearing this burning bread and you are the cup of this wine. O Mary, we earnestly pray to you that, just as water is not divided from wine, so we may not separate ourselves from your son, the lamb of salvation.[22]

And so it is to Mary's son, the newborn Lamb of God, that we now turn.

FIVE

The Birth of Jesus

"She gave birth to her first-born son and wrapped him in swaddling cloths, and laid him in a manger" (Luke 2:7). This is God, finally visible in that very small, tender encircling of this mother's arms around her newborn son. Mary must have felt exhaustion and yet joy, relief mixed with sheer delight. Finally, after months of waiting, praying, and arduous labor, she had done it. Or it had happened to her, in her, and now out of her but so very close to her. "Let it be to me" had finally come to be.

Madeleine L'Engle suggests that Jesus's first cry sounded "like a bell."[1] That cry, which every parent in all of history has welcomed as the happiest of all sorrowful sounds, was echoed in Jesus's name. Angels had told both Mary and Joseph, "You shall call his name Jesus" (Matt. 1:21; Luke 1:31). The Hebrew name *Yeshuʻa* was a popular one. No wonder: it meant "Lord, help!" How many mothers, Mary included, had screamed this prayer during the agonies of labor? And then Jesus, little *Yeshuʻa*, whose mother had pleaded for divine aid, cried out himself for his mother's aid or anybody's really. Humanity's eternal cry for help, echoed and then ultimately answered in this small one, *Yeshuʻa*, Lord, help.

In his two *The Adoration of the Shepherds* paintings, Rembrandt was theologically shrewd to capture the stillness, light and shadow, love and adoration, holiness and revelation surrounding the infant

Alte Pinakothek, Munich, Germany / Bridgeman Images

FIGURE 3. *The Adoration of the Shepherds*, 1646 (oil on canvas), by Rembrandt Harmensz van Rijn (1606–69)

Jesus's first moments (see fig. 3). Rembrandt portrayed Jesus as luminous, glowing like a lantern, illuminating the faces of everyone gathered around. A lovely medieval tradition suggests that when Jesus was born, a hush fell over all the earth for a full hour; even dogs did not bark. Thus the carol, "Silent night, holy night, all is calm." In the fullness of time, the hidden purpose of the words "be still, and know that I am God" (Ps. 46:10) was realized.

Of all the words of Scripture that came to mind, none were as poignant and fitting as those everyone had puzzled over for centuries: "Behold, a virgin shall conceive, and bear a son, and shall call his name Immanuel" (Isa. 7:14 KJV)—the first of many nicknames that would be given to Jesus, meaning simply "God with us." Did Jesus allude to this at the end of his life when he pledged, "I am with you always" (Matt. 28:20)? "God with us" encapsulates God's holy purpose, for it is not merely "God with me" or "God with them" but really "God with us, all of us."

Show Us God

When the boy Jesus had grown up, during his final meal with his closest friends, one of them asked, "Show us the Father, and we shall be satisfied" (John 14:8). Jesus would show them the broken heart of God the Father the next day as he hung on the cross. And he had already shown them the joyful heart of God the Father on day one as he lay in the manger. This is God. At that final meal, Jesus spoke mysteriously of birth once more: "When a woman is in travail she has sorrow, because her hour has come; but when she is delivered of the child, she no longer remembers the anguish, for joy that a child is born into the world. So you have sorrow now, but I will see you again and your hearts will rejoice" (16:21–22). God thought, I want them to know me—so I will do *this*. I will be born and tenderly embraced by my mother, just like all of them. Can you find yourself in that holy circle of Mary's arms enfolding her newborn Jesus? Like Jesus, you once were in such a tender, curled-up circle. You've never been closer to God, or more like God, since this is the way God showed us God's heart.

Consider God's options. God could have rained down brimstone or floated down bags of gold or pretty flowers. God could have remained aloof in heaven, ineffable, invisible, omnipresent, omniscient, omnipotent—the list of *omni*s could go on and on. But God's love could not be contained by all those *omnis*, not even by the limitless expanse of heaven. God had to make it personal to be God. God could have descended, fully grown, muscular, wielding a flashing sword, with an entourage of warriors trailing in his wake. Multitudes would have cheered. But God knew that while the powerful might be feared, they mostly engender intimidation. What God wanted from us was love, tenderness, and compassion. You might want Achilles on your side in the trenches of war. But Achilles always has his Achilles' heel: he elicits terror, not affectionate love.

Martin Luther, who was riddled with intense fear and anxiety about God for so long, put it best: "Behold Christ lying in the lap of his young mother. . . . You cannot fear him, for nothing is more appealing to man than a babe. Are you affrighted? Then come to him, lying in the lap of the fairest and sweetest maid. You will see how great is the divine goodness, which seeks above all else that you should not despair."[2] We don't have to defy gravity and ascend to God; God has descended to us. He reigns, not from a palace but from a manger, just as he will eventually ride a donkey instead of a stallion and wear plaited thorns instead of a bejeweled crown. His craft is not power but love, his entourage not regiments but the riffraff, really anyone who gets and wants love instead of distance and fear.

The Infant Jesus Reborn

It is as if each generation needs to make the stunning rediscovery of the infant Jesus that Saint Francis made. Christendom knew nothing about manger scenes until 1223, when Saint Francis asked a friend in Greccio to arrange things around a cave: a straw crib, oxen, donkeys, and an image of the infant Jesus. The townspeople gathered on Christmas Eve bearing torches. The friars sang medieval carols. Try to imagine their voices echoing from the mountain's edge down through the valley. Try to imagine Saint Francis's voice. On that night, overcome with emotion, he preached—and listeners said his voice sounded like the bleating of a lamb. He picked up the infant figure, held it in his arms, and some said they thought they saw the child come to life. Saint Francis's devotion to the humanity of Christ was tender. God became small, vulnerable, inviting us to love, and to be as tender as God's own heart, power redefined as affection and song.

The point might have been lost on Christendom had it not been for the genius of Giotto di Bondone, whose frescoes captured the emotion, tenderness, humility, and love not only of Saint Francis's life but of Christ's as well. Before Giotto, the infant Christ had always been depicted as a curiously diminutive potentate, with regalia, exuding strength and authority; he was sometimes even muscular. Giotto understood Saint Francis's vision, and he painted Christ for the first time as Christ was once upon a time: small, dependent, vulnerable, and pleading quietly for nothing but love.

No wonder Jesus's birth has stimulated theologians to heights of eloquence. They use the theological term *incarnation*, a terrific word meaning "en-fleshed." In Christ, God unites with our flesh—but why? Gregory Nazianzen, in the fourth century, explained that "what is unassumed is unredeemed."[3] God assumes our fleshy life to redeem it. This was no last-ditch measure, as if other divine efforts at salvation had failed. From the moment of creation, it was always in God's mind and heart to do this: "In the beginning was the Word" (John 1:1). God created humanity in God's image, and it is Jesus who is the very image of God, the true image of who we are, might be, and surely will become. Paul taught that God "emptied himself" (Phil. 2:7) by enduring crucifixion, of course, but also in the nativity of Christ. Listen to Scottish theologian Thomas Torrance: "He the eternal Word of God, the Lord of heaven, stooped down to our low estate stripped of the effulgence of his glory that our weak eyes might behold him in the meek and lowly Jesus, and in and through Jesus be lifted up to the divine glory."[4] Or to revel in the words of another great writer, Annie Dillard: "Faith would be that God . . . bound himself to time and its hazards and haps as a man would lash himself to a tree for love. That God's works are as good as we make them. That God is helpless, our baby to bear, self-abandoned on the doorstep of time, wondered at by cattle and oxen. Faith would be that God moved and moves once and for all and 'down,' so to speak, like a diver."[5]

Theologians can use big words like *effulgence*, and poets may envision God "self-abandoned on the doorstep of time," and we find ourselves thunderstruck and moved. But the truth of the matter is mundane and simple, graspable by a child. Do you want to know God? Look no further than your own birth. God took up residence in a young woman's womb, grew, felt the tremendous press of her labor, and then emerged as all infants emerge into the shock of light, cold, and air. Did Joseph catch him? Someone did—just as someone caught you. Smallness and vulnerability define our God's ultimate self-revelation and offer of love.

The Day the Revolution Began

By engaging in this daring risk of coming to us as a fragile infant, God accepted the potential downside: he might not survive Herod's hysterical rage. He might die young, like so many children did back then. He might be trivialized, as happens with little ones. We coo "How cute!" at infant photos or at a baptism. God, by being born, anticipated the very notion that God taking on flesh would be scandalous, that God would be the laughingstock among the world's religions.

N. T. Wright calls Good Friday "the day the revolution began"— but wasn't it actually Christmas? Being born, Christ jumped into the fray, and nothing was the same. Even on Good Friday, Jesus prayed Psalm 22 (which his mother taught him when he was a boy!), which includes this prayer:

> Yet it was you who took me from the womb.
> . . . .
> On you I was cast from my birth
>   and since my mother bore me you have been my God.
>   (vv. 9–10 NRSV)

Mary, like Jesus, knew these words by heart, and their hearts were both broken and uplifted by them.

A medieval carol we still sing articulates what Mary did on God's behalf: "To show God's love a-right, / she bore to us a Savior, / when half spent was the night."[6] We get God's love a-wrong so easily, fantasizing of a God who is indulgent, chafing under a God whose love is stingy or partial or busying ourselves being good enough for a God who doles out rewards or griping when God proves to be a lousy protection blanket or minding our own business and assuming God is remote. To these and all other ways God is shown wrongly, God says, "Look to the very small, vulnerable one, the one with the theological nickname."

God with Us

Immanuel. God with us. The theologian Sam Wells wisely suggested that the most important word in the Bible and in all of theology is "with."[7] What? A mere preposition? Notice how ubiquitous in Scripture is this notion: the very nature of God is about being with us. From the call of Moses through the eloquence of Isaiah and the Psalms to the exiles in the fiery furnace, God is with Israel. In fact, during the exile, when Israel was banished to far-away Babylon and when God was doing no obvious work for the people, Israel discovered the wonder and even joy of God's surprising yet non-rescuing presence.

This "with" defines the Gospel story. From the birth of Immanuel to his parting words at the ascension, God-in-Christ's mission was to be with us. We may love the Gospel stories of Jesus's miracles; but those are brief snapshots in an otherwise undramatic life, in which Jesus simply lived—as God incarnate!—among regular people in their daily routine; he was simply with them. Wells is right: "Jesus is Immanuel before he is Savior. By overcoming our isolation, Jesus saves us: his death is the cost of that. . . . Both the devil and the mockers goad Jesus with his apparent inactivity. . . . He outlasted humanity's hatred, cruelty and enmity. . . . We want the Jesus that comes down from the cross, the Jesus that rights wrongs, ends pain, corrects injustice. . . . We want solutions, we want our problems fixed." But, on closer inspection, "what humankind needs is a love that sticks around, a love that stays put, a love that hangs on. That's what the cross is. A love that hangs on."[8] God in Christ began hanging on when he began hanging around at his birth.

If God's great revelation to us, God's most decisive act for us is simply being with us, then our relationship with God looks very different, and the Christian life and the mission of the church are forever redefined. God asks us to be with others, not to treat them as projects or problems to be fixed. Parents are wise to understand their children as mysteries, wonders, peculiar, not pliable to strategies or quests to hammer them into the image we fantasize of in our minds. All love is about being with—as Jean Vanier reminds us: "To love someone is not to do things *for* them, but to reveal to them their beauty and value, to say 'You are beautiful. You are important. I trust you. You can trust yourself.' We all know well that we can do things for others and in the process crush them, making them feel that they are incapable of doing things by themselves. To love someone is to reveal to them the light that is shining in them."[9] And thus the mission of God's church is forever redirected, calmed down, and invigorated. We are not asked to do things for people—either to send them aid anonymously, or even to help them, haves to have-nots, directly. Wells clarifies that since Jesus came to be with us, not merely to fix us or right all wrongs, then it is ours to be with others. In his wonderful book *A Nazareth Manifesto*, he writes:

> Our purpose, our calling is to be with God and with one another. . . . There is no goal beyond restored relationship; being with is not a means to an end. . . . We do not sit and have coffee with a homeless person because we are trying to solve their problem. . . . Continue to see the face of Jesus in the despised and rejected of the world. You are not their benefactor. You are not the answer to their prayer. They are the answer to yours. You are searching for a salvation that only they can bring.[10]

Christmas Is Not Your Birthday

And so, since we are exploring the birth of Jesus, can we intuit how this Jesus who is Immanuel, God with us, might alter the way we celebrate Christmas? Most Christians chuckle and acknowledge that Jesus would be mortified by all the commercialism—but then we proceed to the mall and put a "Jesus is the reason for the season" sticker on the back of the van. As veteran pastor Mike Slaughter pointedly reminds us, "Christmas is not *your* birthday"[11]—although we act as if we are the Christ child and expect the magi to deliver fabulous gifts to . . . us. We put on the good face and assuage whatever tinge of guilt might linger by little acts of charity, a spasm of doing good for others. 'Tis the season.

But in Jesus, God was and is with us. God didn't rain down gold coins on Mary. God stuck around, ate, walked, slept, listened, worked with his hands, sang, went to synagogue, dealt with siblings, got sick and well again, grieved those suffering and dying—including Joseph. If this was Jesus's way, then to mark his birth, perhaps we should find ways not to do things for those we love but to focus on being with them. Perhaps instead of helping those in need, we befriend them, realizing our own need and brokenness, and together share in the healing power of God's presence in our togetherness, as God is with us as we are with one another.

And God is with *all* the one anothers. Reflecting on those who fret over a culture not as attached to Jesus during December as they would like it to be, Sarah Howell, in a thoughtful sermon, reminds us that "Jesus wasn't born only for those who keep Christ in Christmas. Jesus was born for everyone. . . . Jesus came for love of all humanity long before anyone knew or professed his name. We forget that Jesus was unable to speak his own name. We forget that Jesus came, not teaching and admonishing, but wailing, hungry, human."[12]

A fascinating, charming, and theologically meaningful element in the way we think of the birth of Jesus is the presence of the animals. We cannot imagine manger scenes without the animals we sing about: "The cattle are lowing"; "where ox and ass are feeding"; "said the night wind to the little lamb." The song "The Friendly Beasts" even features speeches for the donkey "shaggy and brown," the cow "all white and red," the sheep "with curly horn," and the dove "from the rafters high." Edward Hicks created several *Peaceable Kingdom* paintings involving wolves and lambs, bulls and infants lounging placidly together—inspired, of course, by Isaiah 11's vision of such a day. When Saint Francis created his manger scene in Greccio, he ordered that all the animals be given a double portion of food—this from Saint Francis, famous for fasting. Jesus, after all, was laid in a manger—a stone feeding trough for animals.

How fitting. It's as if God anticipated that I would shrivel God's plan down to nothing more than my personal salvation, or even God helping me when I'm in a bind. The Bible, clearly and consistently, dreams a far more expansive dream: the redemption of the entire created order, including animals, plant life, and the earth itself. Creation isn't to be swept away but redeemed; Richard Middleton calls this "the Bible's best-kept secret."[13] We may relish the idea that our golden retriever will join us in heaven; but God made, loves, and surely will redeem badgers, blowfish, rodents, and those annoying birds that peck away at your garden.

Redeeming Time and Place

To press the implications of the birth of this humble child even further: the narratives in Matthew and Luke take pains to pinpoint the historical time and geographic place of Jesus's birth. Madeleine L'Engle penned a poem declaring that

> He did not wait till the world was ready,
> till men and nations were at peace.
> He came when the Heavens were unsteady,
> and prisoners cried out for release.
>
> He did not wait for the perfect time.
> He came when the need was deep and great.
> . . . .
> To a world like ours, of anguished shame
> he came, and his Light would not go out.[14]

We cannot interview God and ask for an explanation of the timing.

And yet, how provocative. The Savior arrived during what was arguably history's greatest empire. He arrived during the reign of the greatest and most powerful of all the rulers, a mighty emperor without peer, one who pledged peace and bounty—Caesar Augustus. The Savior also arrived during the tenure of Caesar's great friend, the most notorious, potent, and cruel of Judea's kings—the frightening and dastardly Herod the Great. Luke's telling of things clearly puts a stake in the ground: all the pompous promises spouting from this great Caesar Augustus would falter, and only the humble child that

Caesar never even heard of would be the real deal; Herod crushed almost all his foes, but this one child would slip through his fingers and rule humbly, gently, and eternally.

You would think God would have waited for an easier moment, maybe during the chaotic, wimpy reigns of Otho or Galba. But no. Perhaps, just as Moses (a mere baby in a basket) managed to rescue Israel from Egypt during the reign of Rameses the Great, the greatest of all the pharaohs, so God shrewdly began God's invasive, subversive work during the time the opposition was at its most ferocious, when the empire felt utterly impregnable.

God in Christ came to redeem time, the time in which each of us is born, and to redeem place, all the places where we arrive and live out our days. As Luke relates the story, it looked like Jesus would be born in Nazareth—a fitting and holy choice, as God seemed to delight in whatever was unexpected, unlikely, and humble. But a better idea emerged: the "little town of Bethlehem."

Why Bethlehem? The Bible's authors care that the Messiah is born in the city of David, from whose lineage the ultimate king of Israel must come. Curiously, as much as any place, Bethlehem is situated at the intersection of the continents, or at least most of them (and those that are not connected to Bethlehem by land now once were in the recesses of geological history).

Drive to Bethlehem today. You'll arrive at a heavily guarded checkpoint. The security station is manned by stern police with an array of concrete barriers, and watchtowers loom over your head with sharpshooters positioned and ready. The world-famous wall, designed to keep peace, is at its most imposing in Bethlehem. And that wall is adorned with remarkable graffiti, some from well-known artists like Banksy and Lushsux, including a dove wearing a flak jacket and a soldier hurling not a grenade but a bouquet of flowers. On the wall are placards where mothers simply tell their stories—of sons and husbands killed in the seemingly never-ending struggles between Israel and Palestine. Jesus was born in a contested place— back then and today—a place where redemption seems impossible. We are invited to recall Gabriel's response to Mary: "For with God nothing will be impossible" (Luke 1:37); the shepherds heard the angels hovering above this place, singing of peace (2:14).

The history of this town is instructive. The prophet Samuel visited there to anoint the next king of Israel, who was to be among Jesse's sons. After surveying the lineup of seven young men, Samuel finally realized it was David, the one Jesse had left out in the field, who would be the anointed one, illustrating the theological maxim that similarly explains the birth of Jesus—that God sees not as we see (1 Sam. 16:7).

Fast forward two millennia from the time of Samuel, Jesse, and David. Christian crusaders, led by Tancred, seized Bethlehem from the Arabs, touching off a century of skirmishes. Saint Francis of Assisi may have visited the town during these days. But more importantly, he created that first manger scene, a replica of Bethlehem, back in Italy. That very year, crusaders were in combat with Arabs, vying for control of the original Bethlehem. Chiara Frugoni suggests that Saint Francis was saying we do not need to fight to get to Bethlehem. Any place, Greccio or the town where you are reading this, can be Bethlehem.[15]

How fascinating, our manger scenes. History has bequeathed great personalities to us. Abraham Lincoln was born in a one-room log cabin in Hodgenville, Kentucky; William Shakespeare was born in a Tudor house in Stratford-upon-Avon; and Harriet Tubman was born in slave quarters in Madison, Maryland. But we do not fashion a log cabin, a Tudor house, or a slave hovel in the front yard or on the mantel to commemorate their lives. The birth of Jesus pervades time and space and is evoked in tangible ways in countless places, as every place is meant to be redeemed by the birth of this child.

Lest we get too sentimental about it, we may shiver a little when we read Rowan Williams's suggestive words about the Christ-child: "The Burning Babe, who has come to cast fire upon the earth. Before his presence, the idols fall and shatter."[16]

SIX

Jesus's First Days

What was Jesus's very early life like, his first few hours, days, and weeks? We love the carol that says, "Little Lord Jesus, no crying he makes." But surely he cried. We should hope he cried. He became one with all of us who cry. Babies cry, and we may be grateful, as that sound is the sign of life and vitality, a protest against being so rudely removed from the warm safety of the womb, a dual declaration to the world: "I have arrived" and "Something's wrong." As an adult, Jesus wept over the city of Jerusalem and over the death of his friend Lazarus, and he surely still weeps over us. As discussed before, Jesus's very name is a cry, *Yeshu'a,* meaning "Lord, help!"

Mary nursed him, rocked him, whispered and sang to him. Like all mothers, she fought through the weariness. Did she suffer any postpartum depression? Like all parents, Mary and Joseph spoke to their child, which is how Jesus, the Word made flesh, learned both to speak and to listen. What was Jesus's first word? How lovely would it be to learn that, one day, little Jesus uttered his first intelligible word—and that it was "Abba," the easiest of all words to utter, meaning "Daddy." This word would have been used by Jesus to speak with Joseph, it was used by Jesus as an adult when he prayed to God in heaven, and it was used by Paul, who urges us to use it when praying our toughest, most intimate prayers (Rom. 8:15).

In Jesus's early life, there were many visits. The shepherds flocked to his manger, perplexed and overstimulated by what they swore they'd seen and heard out in the fields: angels trumpeting and singing. And if they correctly heard the angels (who must have spoken and sung in Hebrew!), a revolution was beginning: this good news was not just for them or their town folk or even their nation but for "all the people" (Luke 2:10). And the pledge was not that a great warrior was about to annihilate their foes. No, this one was to usher in peace on earth (Luke 2:14).

We may have heard that these shepherds were poor, hapless, and homeless. But many shepherds ran thriving businesses. Unlike the magi, they brought Jesus no gifts—except their curiosity and their joyful hearts, which are always the best gifts parents receive when a child has been born.

The magi appeared in due course, right away or months later, we have no way of knowing—just as we don't know how many of them made the trek from Persia or Arabia or wherever. We guess there were three, since they delivered three gifts; but artists have depicted four or seven or a dozen.

We fixate on their gifts and what they symbolize (the myrrh being the dark one, hinting at Jesus's suffering to come). But the holy humor is that the magi figured out where to go. These magi were astrologers. Back then, Jewish and then later Christian theologians regarded the craft of astrology as invalid and even demonic. And yet the magi found the child, while Herod's Scripture scholars missed it all. Those who think they know God best so often can't grasp what's right in front of them. Or up in the night sky. There's nothing this God won't resort to, so eager is God to be found by any- and everybody.

Mary and Joseph were, of course, thoroughly Jewish, and their Jewishness shaped the world into which Jesus woke up in his earliest days. When Mary sang, she sang psalms; she knew them by heart. "By heart": I love the way we know words to certain songs without look- ing because such songs resonate deeply in the part of us that dreams, loves, misses, and yearns. What we know by heart is cultivated over more than a single lifetime: it's generational, genealogical, cultural. Aren't lullabies like that? Jesus came into the crucible of the Jewish world, in the home of King David himself, to parents immersed in

Israel's Scriptures, which they knew by heart and then Jesus did as well. So together they inherited God's historic and eternal mission for the chosen people to be God's instrument to rescue the world from exile and participate in the revolution of the redemption of all of creation.

Handing Him Over for the First Time

Mary, on cue, did as all Jewish mothers did: she and her family made the arduous journey (with a newborn!) to Jerusalem for her "purification" (Luke 2:21–24). We might wonder why she of all mothers would need to be purified. But having just borne God's own son, she stuck to the law, seeking to be as pure and holy as possible in God's eyes—perhaps akin to the way Jesus, God in the flesh, holiest of the holy, submitted to baptism. And as pious, observant Jews, hardly done with the Torah now that Jesus has arrived, Jesus's parents offered up a couple of sacrificial birds on the altar. Those "two turtledoves" made it into the eighteenth-century carol "The Twelve Days of Christmas."

And then, being diligent in faith, Mary and Joseph delivered their son to the priest for circumcision, which for them was a nonnegotiable act of obedience and devotion to God. I wonder whether Mary felt her first pangs of separation when she handed her infant son over to a priest she'd never met and whether she shivered when she heard Jesus's cry when the knife cut into his flawless flesh.

Seemingly by chance, Mary and Joseph bumped into an old man named Simeon, and then a woman named Anna who had been a widow for decades (Luke 2:25–38). The aged inevitably turn and gaze at an infant, as if the chances to glimpse such precious beauty are numbered—as George Eliot noted when telling us about the reclusive miser, Silas Marner, who discovered a little girl in his home after losing all his gold: "We older human beings feel a certain awe in the presence of a little child, such as we feel before some quiet majesty or beauty in earth or sky."[1] Do mothers today encounter various older people who figure in profound and surprising ways in the unfolding

Public Domain

FIGURE 4. *Presentation of Christ in the Temple*, 1302–5, by Giotto di Bondone (1266–1337)

drama of their children's lives? Does God send such people into our orbit to shape the puzzled parents' new world?

Simeon was "righteous and devout." Like many, he was "looking for the consolation of Israel" (Luke 2:25). Some mystical disclosure had come to this man—that he would not die before seeing the Messiah. Simeon took the child. Mary would forever be handing her child over to the hopes of others. His prayer over the child must have struck Mary and Joseph dumb. "Now let your servant depart in peace," for this Messiah (even in infancy) had come, "a light for revelation to the Gentiles, and for glory to your people Israel" (vv. 29, 32 RSV alt.). We often speak hyperbolically of a newborn, but this is over the top, either divinely inspired or sheer craziness. Such a lovely hope though, that because of this child we might depart in peace. No wonder monks and nuns chant these words each night.

Would that Simeon had stopped right there. But then, in somber tones, he spoke directly to Mary: "Behold, this child is set for the fall and rising of many in Israel. . . . A sword will pierce through your own soul" (Luke 2:34–35). These densely framed words require much thought; we can be sure that Mary "pondered" them. Her little boy's destiny involves the "fall and rising" of God's people. The order should puzzle us. We speak of the "rise and fall" of, let's say, the Roman Empire, a British dynasty, or a famous politician. With Jesus, everything gets turned upside down. With Jesus, you fall before you rise, you are emptied of your own goodness before you are filled with the mercy, you lose your life to gain your life—and the same happens with God's church, rising like a phoenix only after suffering the worst persecution.

The pattern will be Jesus's own. He will fall, flagellated by the soldiers. He will carry his own cross and finally be crushed by death itself, only then to rise and reign. This fall will indeed pierce Mary's soul. Simeon was right: she would barely be able to stand at the foot of the cross, trying to avert her gaze from the sight of the lifeblood she had given him draining out of his precious, pure body. But she had to watch and love and grieve. Whose heart was more crushed than hers? Who felt the piercing of the nails and the spear more than his mother? Who, even after his resurrection and ascension, felt the pangs of missing him more than his holy mother?

The Power of Prophecies

Simeon's prophecy may prompt us to consider all the prophecies, most of them surely unintended, uttered over our children. Sizing up mom and dad, the doctor says, "He'll be a tall one!" Or as a preemie beats the odds, the nurse says, "She's a fighter!" Or as the too-young mother labors, with no family nearby, the obstetrician hangs her head, "That one is already behind the eight ball." Saint Dominic's mother, Juana, traveled to Silos in Castile while she was still pregnant. In the sanctuary she had a vision: a little dog was in her womb, with a blazing torch in his mouth, setting the world on fire. Rebekah's twins writhed in her womb, foreshadowing the vicious sibling rivalry that was to come (Gen. 25:22–23).

Were there prophecies you've overheard about yourself? I have vague recollections that when my sister was born my parents declared that they had really wanted a boy. So I was their boy! And she was not. . . . Other prophecies are cute but loaded. We purchased Duke bibs and socks for our wee ones—so did they feel they failed to fulfill their promise when they didn't go to Duke? Some prophetic messages that impact our children are entirely unnoticed and unspoken—like parental anxiety over what to do with a little one or over how terribly scary the world is.

A parent's own childhood can function as a prophecy for the new child just born. In *Parenting from the Inside Out*, Daniel Siegel and Mary Hartzell demonstrate how our brains are wired so that when we parent, we quite naturally re-create the emotional interactions and responses experienced when we were little. You're weighed down by unacknowledged emotional baggage. Your child triggers a response in you that's way more about that hidden baggage than about the present situation—and then everybody winds up confused, upset, and overwhelmed. Worst of all, your child then grows up and repeats the pattern with his or her own child.

Evil Recoiling

Speaking of the prophetic, remember those long shadows in Rembrandt's *The Adoration of the Shepherds*? Immediately upon Jesus's birth, history's ongoing struggle of good versus evil was ratcheted up quite a few notches. Some views of Christmas might elicit warm feelings over the picture of Jesus's parents with their sweet child. But a cosmic battle had just begun. "Why do the nations rage?" the psalmist asks (Ps. 2:1 KJV alt.). Upon Jesus's birth, the idolatrous, unholy powers seem to realize that their domain has been invaded.

And so they recoiled—like that haunting moment in Peter Jackson's film version of *The Fellowship of the Ring*. The wicked "eye of

Sauron," atop a high tower, casts its evil beam over the land, probing, ruling, intimidating, always watching for signs of good to be dealt with; "its wrath blazed like a sudden flame and its fear was like a great black smoke, for it knew its deadly peril, the thread upon which hung its doom."[2] When Frodo put on the ring of power, the eye was seized with some paroxysm of envy and terror, jerking suddenly in Frodo's direction, far away. Jesus was born quietly, many miles from Herod or Caesar Augustus. But in that moment, there was a recoil, a leap to secure the borders and to police the people so the ruling powers would remain unchecked. How astonishing that this birth struck anxiety into the hearts of those dwelling arrogantly and securely in the corridors of power.

An appalling, gruesome manifestation of this evil recoil was unleashed by King Herod. Notorious for his paranoia, famously feeling threatened by and then killing members of his own family, Herod flew into what was for him a typical rage, ordering the cruel slaughter of all male boys under the age of two in his realm. The arrival of the Christ child was no security blanket to shelter the people from harm. On the contrary, his advent actually brought on intense sorrow, such is the ferocious, knee-jerk retaliation of evil against the good that would bring life—back then and throughout history.

The laments, the shrieks of the mothers of Judea have echoed through time. If we listen, we can still hear them and all mothers who have crumpled to the ground in agony as they have witnessed violence against their children. A mother, wrenched from her small son in Auschwitz, was forced to watch with the rest of the horrified crowd as he dangled by a rope around his neck. A man in the crowd asked, "For God's sake, where is God?" Elie Wiesel, who was there, said he heard a voice answer, "This is where—hanging here from this gallows."[3]

It is a painful thing to grow deep in the faith. When faith is small, it is easy to live in a bubble, grateful that our child is here, safe, cozy. But a larger, broader faith draws us into solidarity with others. We may be safe, but the Christian mother realizes she is in a sorority with mothers who live at great risk, who suffer much, whose agony is unspeakable, incurable. Right away Mary knew, loved, and was one with other mothers who wailed in unutterable pain.

Of course, thanks to a good angel who warned Joseph, by stealth Jesus's family fled to Egypt. Legend has it that lions and leopards in the wilderness bowed their heads and wagged their tails in homage. Palm trees bent low to provide food for them. Two thieves pounced on them but then relented when Mary wept—the same robbers who were crucified next to Jesus thirty years later.[4] The symbolism of this flight to Egypt would not have been lost on the Jews of Jesus's day or on careful Bible readers today. This child, who came to deliver the people, descended to Egypt, as Joseph and his brothers had centuries earlier, only to return in peace to the land of promise.

Still in his infancy, Jesus was a refugee, joining the ranks of countless throngs of people through history who have been pushed out of their homelands, desperate to survive grisly armies, rulers, and thugs. I have known Jews who managed to slip out of Europe and elude the Nazis; a neighbor of mine was hidden in a potato sack and thrown onto the back of a truck by her parents, whom she never saw again. Refugee camps dot the globe. Particularly haunting are the refugee camps now located where Jesus was born. Near Bethlehem itself, camps like Dheisheh and Aida have been home to thousands of Palestinians refugees, who have lived in harsh conditions for generations, since the war in 1948.

We shudder when we consider Herod's slaughter of the innocents and the sufferings that the Herods of the world have inflicted on so many. Even in safer circumstances, every parent knows that a child can't be sequestered from harm. There will be inevitable wounds, physical and emotional. Jesus also had his childhood wounds, since he was one of us. One of the early gospels that didn't make it into the canon, "The Infancy Gospel of Thomas," regales us with a far-fetched story that I'm fond of: When Jesus was a little boy, a playmate poked fun at him; the boy laughed at Jesus and called him names. Very childishly, Jesus waved a finger and struck the boy dead; then, feeling holy remorse, he raised the boy back to life.

I bet Jesus was made fun of by other kids; surely he felt the angst, awkwardness, and shame I felt, and perhaps you felt, as a child. If I'd had divine power, I would have struck down those who bullied me. On second thought, I would have cast some spell and made them play with me, pick me first for kickball, and maybe love me.

After that quick visit to Jerusalem for purification and circumcision, the Bible tells us nothing at all about Jesus's childhood until he is twelve years old—beyond the scope of what we're discussing in this book. But that moment is instructive. The holy family made their way to Jerusalem as part of a caravan of travelers from Nazareth to enjoy the high festival days in Jerusalem. Headed for home, somehow Jesus was misplaced; his parents couldn't locate him for three days. Once they did, Mary upbraided him: "Son, why have you treated us so? Behold, your father and I have been looking for you anxiously" (Luke 2:48). Indeed. Even they were learning what all religiously serious parents learn: you do not know what God is calling your child to become, which raises the question of why we have children in the first place.

PART 3

THE COMPLEXITIES OF CONCEPTION AND RAISING CHILDREN

SEVEN

Why Have Children?

If you want your life turned inside out, try being the parent of the infant undergoing birth, that most radical of transitions. One day you're a human being of considerable independence. Nine months later, your body has been transmuted into something previously unknown. Your emotions are titillated or wrecked. You don't just pop down the street or go to the movies without considerable planning and packing up of kiddie items. You're grateful for three hours of sleep. You worry in ways you'd never thought possible. Even if it's child number two or three, having a child is a universe-changer.

This is fascinating: parents have nine months to get ready, to read books, and to brace for the changes. They hear lots of stories and wisdom from family and friends. And yet almost all new parents report how surprised they are once it all unfolds. The bombshell that birth is for the parents is too great for words, although the poet John O'Donohue offers us a few in his poem "For a Mother-to-Be":

> Nothing could have prepared
> Your heart to open like this.[1]

I recall clearly that my expectations of how I might feel when we finally had our child in our arms were overrun by reality. I kept telling anybody who would listen, "I love this child more than I thought possible." Mind you, people experience a broad range of feelings on this. The jolt of emotion that is childbirth can plunge a mom into the dark abyss of postpartum depression, ushering in the worst kind of isolation because everyone around can't imagine that having a child could elicit anything but delight.

Theologically, we should say that the parents (and this always involves both of them, even if one has vacated the premises) have shared with God in fashioning yet one more human being who we believe is created in God's very own image. "In the image of God he created them; male and female he created them" (Gen. 1:27 NRSV)—and after the first humans, God does so through human agency or not at all. Madeleine L'Engle articulated how this is no small thing: "It takes two to make the image of God. It takes all aspects of ourselves to be part of that image."[2] Everything about mom and dad that matters—their DNA, their hearts and minds, their sexual selves—is poured into this new life.

No wonder the change feels so drastic. Parents muster every fiber of their being to nurture this other person who isn't really "other" at all. The Bible speaks of the old passing away and God doing a new thing, of us being some kind of new creature in Christ (Isa. 43:18–19; 2 Cor. 5:17). When in life do you sense the loss of the old self and the dawning of a new self so much as after the birth of your child? This identity origami may have begun during pregnancy, especially for the mom; as O'Donohue puts it, "Once it began, you were no longer your own."[3] This emergence of a new self, not just for this child but also for the grownups involved, this new courage and ability to sacrifice isn't anticipated, is it? I mean, that's not why you have children—to increase your character scores on courage and sacrifice. If you want to learn courage and the glory of humanity, look to the parents with intense challenges. Brian Doyle tells about a child born without any limbs. The parents were mortified and turned away, but the nurse at hand adopted the child. She and her husband thought their adopted daughter was "the best Gift ever." After the little girl died four years later, the nurse and her husband adopted more children, prompting Doyle to exclaim, "There really are couples like that on this planet."[4]

The Big Adventure

Why do we have children? I can confess that somehow, well into adulthood and despite being a nerdy, curious person, I had never given much thought to the question, "Why have children?" I guess I assumed I would want to marry and have a couple of them one day, because . . . I'd not tried to fill in the blank. Is it just innate? When we mate, we enact our close kinship to the chimpanzees, beetles, orangutans, penguins, porpoises, pigs, porcupines, and polecats who similarly mate. Are we seeking fulfillment? Tax credits or welfare checks? Did the birth control simply fail? I overheard my mother telling someone she had me to save her marriage.

How about having a child to save your own life? In Tudor England, women on death row were known to "plead the belly," avoiding execution and buying time for a possible royal pardon; in the mixed-gender prisons of the day, pregnancies happened. Agnes Samuel, a woman already imprisoned for witchcraft, was urged to plead the belly, but she replied that she could not bear being thought both a witch and a whore. Shortly thereafter, she was hanged.[5]

Why have children? To provide someone to love you in your old age? To have more hands to work the farm? To populate your vision of the good life? To fulfill your dreams? Elaine Scarry wrote that "beauty brings copies of itself into being."[6] She was thinking of drawings or photographs, but what if the beauty we are and the beauty we see in one another recrafts itself in a newborn infant? Or are we simply meeting social expectations?

Do we have children to do evolution's bidding—to keep our genes alive? Lance Smith was killed in a car accident. Mysteriously, he had left written instructions urging his fiancée to use his sperm to have a child. She understandably refused, so then his parents sued to secure rights to his sperm so someone else could carry on his (their) family line.[7] Do your genes press you to fulfill their apparent urge for immortality?

Speaking of urges: having a child can be the full-bodied completion of natural sexual attractions. Physical intimacy is marvelous and scary—and might just usher in a new person. God invited humanity to "be fruitful and multiply," leaving vast space for use and misuse of this scintillating potential.

Do we simply like big adventures? Meaghan O'Connell reported that for her and her husband "*pregnant* meant throwing up our hands, giving ourselves over to fate, doing something crazy. It seemed romantic, reckless, wild, like packing up all our stuff and going on a long trip with no itinerary. For twenty years. No, for forever."[8]

The "something crazy" will strike many as great fun. For others, the "crazy" can be dark. No one embarks on the adventure of having a child in order to suffer crippling mental agony. And yet postpartum depression is real, often covered up, and, despite brave women who've demanded a hearing, still poorly understood. In *Maternity, Mortality, and the Literature of Madness*, Marilyn Yalom explores how well-known women writers such as Sylvia Plath, Margaret Atwood, and Virginia Woolf have struggled with intense apprehension, fears of death, and mental breakdown when it comes to procreation. Sarah Porten, after coming home with her new baby, began feeling irritable and had to fight off violent thoughts—symptoms she had learned indicated postpartum depression. So she did the right thing: she went to a women's clinic and told her story. The nurse there called the police. A mental health challenge, criminalized.[9]

Later we will explore the agony of wanting children desperately but being unable to achieve a sustained pregnancy and also the most intense of all griefs: the loss of a child. This weightiest potential we have in us, the one most fraught with peril and the possibilities for severe disappointment and unspeakable sorrow: Why even go there? The desire for children in itself can be a kind of torment. The Bible tells stories of childless Hannah being taunted by her rival, Peninnah (1 Sam. 1), and of the desperate lengths Abraham went to with his wife and his concubine and the heartbreak it caused for everyone (Gen. 16).

When we ask, "Why have children?," we should in parallel ask, "Why not have children?" Many couples are childless by choice, and single parenting is in the ascendancy; stigmas around these seem to be lessening over time. Contraception in some religious traditions is a no-no, a violation of nature. And yet the sheer weight of balancing sexual desire versus the possibility of a pregnancy presses even very pious couples into a kind of dual existence: attached and loyal to a church yet ignoring the rules. Contraception is a kind of wisdom that might be a "no" or it might be a "not yet." Why have children now versus later on?

No Such Thing as Reproduction

The one thing we might believe we can do by having children, but most assuredly are not doing, is reproducing. We may refer to reproduction or we speak of reproductive medicine. But as the psychologist Andrew Solomon reminds us in his intriguing book *Far from the Tree*, "There is no such thing as reproduction." What we do is production. Parents fantasize that they will reproduce themselves—or perhaps the best possible version of themselves. But instead "parenthood abruptly catapults us into a permanent relationship with a stranger."[10] Children carry throwback genes and recessive traits; the mix of your and your spouse's genetic codes has unpredictable results. Solomon's study focuses on children who are dwarves, blind, differently abled in various ways and on children who are the result of rape. Solomon tracks how families gradually tolerate, accept, and even celebrate children "who are not what they originally had in mind." And yet the lesson is that "all offspring are startling to their parents; these most dramatic situations are merely variations on a common theme."[11]

Solomon has put a scientifically rigorous face to that well-known Chicken Soup for the Soul fable by Emily Perl Kingsley called "Welcome to Holland."

> When you're going to have a baby, it's like planning a fabulous vacation trip—to Italy. You buy a bunch of guidebooks. . . . You may learn some handy phrases in Italian. It's all very exciting. After months of eager anticipation, the day finally arrives. You pack your bags and off you go. Several hours later, the plane lands. The stewardess comes in and says, "Welcome to Holland." "Holland?!?" you say. "I signed up for Italy! . . . All my life I've dreamed of going to Italy."[12]

Kingsley explains why adjustment after parental disappointment matters: "If you spend your life mourning the fact that you didn't get to Italy, you may never be free to enjoy the very special, the very lovely things . . . about Holland."[13]

Birth quite truly transports you to a new and very different country. Wisdom recognizes and accepts this at the outset. Many parents, beginning in the labor and delivery room, treat the child as The Biggest Project Ever. Photos and videos record every inch of progress. The résumé for college entry is already mapped out. This child will be in the best preschool, will have the best sitter (maybe one who knows Mandarin), and will be afforded all the finest opportunities. We will read the best books every night and ensure no harm comes to this budding superstar. When any challenge rears its head, we will fix it and do so quickly. Feels like the best a parent can do, right?

But you're headed to Holland. Martin Marty gifted us with a fabulous book, *The Mystery of the Child*, whose thesis is, "The provision of care for children will proceed on a radically revised and improved basis if, instead of seeing the child first as a problem faced with a complex of problems, we see her as a mystery surrounded by mystery."[14] Marty continues, "The adult who conceives of the child as having come from an abyss of mystery and who is moving toward another can make more of the moment than those who resort to compiling scrapbooks in order to retain the past or who make all their moves in efforts to ensure lasting outcomes in the future."[15] You're not in Italy, even if you manufacture a childhood that feels like a lovely Tuscan village. You've not reproduced, and you can't. This one entrusted to you is a stranger—or better, a mystery. Be in awe. Let the child be. See what unfolds. Marvel. Be puzzled—and happily so. This child will hear a different drummer. Some musician will sweep her off her feet one day. He'll surprise you by becoming a chef. She might be bored by all you hold dear and traipse off to a seemingly unsafe corner of the globe to save the world. This child is God's, not yours. As Kierkegaard puts it, after pondering Abraham's haunting willingness to sacrifice his beloved son Isaac, "Only he who draws the knife gets Isaac."[16]

The Need to Worship and Adore

So how can we think about birth—and God? Not many embark on the sexual intimacy that is the launching point for parenthood thinking, "In nine months, I will discover God." But for quite a few religious people, and for some who weren't religious previously, this is what unfolds. In chapter 2 we spoke of Dorothy Day, when she was far from the prayerful, very Catholic champion of the poor she would later become. Having gotten pregnant out of wedlock, she described her daughter Tamar's impact on her: "No human creature could receive or contain so vast a flood of love and joy as I often felt after the birth of my child. With this came the need to worship, to adore" (see fig. 5).[17]

FIGURE 5. **Dorothy Day with her daughter, Tamar**

Used with permission of Kate Hennesey

Ask mothers to narrate childbirth. To each teller, her story is unique—and it is. An intensity of emotion, a peculiar turn of events. And then many will add something like "I never felt closer to God." Or "I was so grateful to God." Or "How could anyone think there's not a God?" Of course, many mothers are deeply and emotionally present in such moments and don't connect the dots in this way. And when mothers speak of this witness to God's reality, they are hitching God (for the first of countless times) to the healthy, hoped-for outcome for their child. And yet God isn't God because we enjoy happy outcomes. God is God when there are less fortunate, more daunting outcomes. If there really are parents who adore children with no arms or legs, then there really is a God when such children are born.

Given my job as a pastor, I was overly attuned to offhand remarks during Lisa's pregnancies. Someone would ask, "Is it a boy or a girl?" After shrugging that we didn't know, the person would often say, "Doesn't matter, as long as it's healthy." And I would respond, usually in the privacy of my head, "And we'll love it even if it isn't." If your child is healthy, you know it might have been otherwise; no one can take this for granted.

Here is a test for the faithful: How do you speak of being blessed by the robust health of your child, given the manifold realities of children who are born ill or lacking something on the checklist of all that is "normal"? How do you speak of the blessing of children when you do so always in earshot of others who battle infertility? For much of my life as a pastor, I've wished we would ban use of that troubling word *blessed*, as we use it too blithely to describe how we got exactly what we'd always dreamed of. But *blessed* falls cruelly on the ears of others you know and love whose wishes didn't come true—not to mention on the existence of beautiful people, much loved by God, who live in the world's most harrowing zones where none of our "blessings" ever happen.

Breeding the Resistance

Beyond sensing God's presence in the moment of birth, even in cases where there is a crisis or a tragedy, are there other connections between God and birth? After noting the theological thinness of the reasons many Christians offer for having children, Stanley Hauerwas suggests that "we must recover the moral significance of our willingness to have children. . . . A child represents our willingness to go on in the face of difficulties, suffering, and the ambiguity of modern life and is thus our claim that we have something worthwhile to pass on."[18] We have children because we are captives of hope; we trust God's future.

Or we might reflect on Martin Luther's reasons for getting married. He sent a letter of invitation to George Spalatin that read, "You must come to my wedding. I have made the angels laugh and the devils weep." And to Leonard Kopp he wrote, "I am going to get married. God likes to work miracles, and to make a fool of the world. You must come."[19] How is having a child one more skirmish in our ongoing battle against evil in the world? How can the advent of a family be a witness, a countercultural delight?

What, after all, is the primary purpose of parenting? Jürgen Moltmann suggests that "parents have a messianic function towards their children too, being to a special degree their missionaries and evangelists. Children are not foundlings, so to speak, shut out from their parents' faith and condemned to find it for themselves."[20]

We might now begin to ask questions of calling. At various points in our journey of faith, we are urged to ask, "What is God's call? What is God asking me to do?" What if we relate this to one of the most important crossroads in life: "Is God calling us to have a child?" How could you distinguish such a calling from other reasons to have a child? Is that primal desire a pivotal piece of how God calls you to parenthood? Even if calling wasn't contemplated around the time of conception, could new parents begin to understand what they've waded into as a calling? Clearly this is now our divine vocation; how do we fulfill parenting with a robust sense that all we do is a response to God's call?

Parents who ask about God's call may be more acutely and painfully attuned to the sorrows and struggles in God's world into which we bring children. I have a friend whose son was born the day before the horrific massacre of children at Sandy Hook Elementary School in Newtown, Connecticut. As she watched the news coverage unfold, she kept crying, clinging to her newborn. But this does not mean merely fretting over the peril that is this world or the inevitable griefs that life will bring. (As Thetis uttered to Achilles, "O my poor child, I bore you for sorrow, nursed you for grief."[21]) It also means understanding that we are part of the Body of Christ, those who are called together to be the light to the nations, to be a force against the forces of evil.

I have friends who are politically engaged community activists. When they've had children, they've declared that they are "breeding the resistance." When Jeremiah was called in the womb, his mother (did she hear a call?) was birthing a voice of radical subversion against evil empires. When those gutsy Hebrew midwives, Shiphrah and Puah, disobeyed Pharaoh's orders and let little boys live, they were subverting the harsh dominance of Egypt (Exod. 1:15–21). When Jesus was born, the Romans hardly noticed; but they should have trembled in their boots over the dawning of a rebel movement that would undermine the very foundations of the empire. When a Christian has a child, the Body of those who will labor for good has expanded by one.

Marked Forever

I've not heard any woman say that she wanted to have children so her body would forever be indelibly marked with the evidence. Decades after giving birth, Lisa has a slightly brownish crescent across her abdomen where she not once but three times was cut open while delivering our kids by C-section. Rachel Hollis, TV personality and author of *Girl, Wash Your Face*, posted an Instagram photo of herself that went viral with this caption: "I have stretch marks and I wear a bikini . . . because I'm proud of this body and every mark on it. . . . They aren't scars, ladies, they're stripes and you've earned them."[22] Liberating, this robust view of what women have tried to cover up for centuries.

If you get a tattoo, you choose to be wounded a bit, to be marked forever. Stretch marks, like many wounds, are more accidental but no less telling. I love the insight Graham Greene shared in *The End of the Affair.* A woman notices what used to be a wound on her lover's shoulder and contemplates the advancing wrinkles in his face: "I thought of lines life had put on his face, as personal as a line of writing—I thought of a scar on his shoulder that wouldn't have been there if once he hadn't tried to protect another man from a falling wall. The scar was part of his character, and I knew I wanted that scar to exist through all eternity."[23]

The scars in Jesus's hands and side, earned when he gave life to all of us, were not blotted out by the resurrection (John 20:27). How women come by these character marks is a harrowing wonder.

EIGHT

Having Children

Many mothers, when asked to narrate the weightiest, most intensely personal event in their lives, will choose the birth of their child—even when their experiences ranged from joyous delight to imponderable shudders. While most memorable experiences are focused on just a few minutes, having a child requires up to nine months, and so the zenith of birth has high drama often punctuated with languor, a long wait, space for worry, dreaming, weariness, nesting, and even prayers you've never prayed before.

After the long season of preparation, anticipation, and anxiety, the day finally comes. You're having a baby. Today. It never seems to be on the "due date," as if to dispel any illusions of control. As Anne Lamott writes, "If you want to make God laugh, tell her your plans."[1]

Interestingly, the way we try to articulate the miracle, the horror, the wonder, and the agony of childbirth sounds very much like what life with Christ is like—or could be like. When we talk about the narrowly focused intensity of giving birth to a child, we echo what the Bible suggests life with Christ is like, yet mercifully thinned out over a lifetime. Listen to Angela Garbes, and think about how Jesus speaks of the way of the cross: "Childbirth is beautiful, but it is not pretty. It is grisly and life affirming, glorious and deadly. It requires you to open, to rip apart both physically and emotionally and allows the scent of death to seep through

96

those tears and fissures."[2] Or ponder Anne Enright's recollection of having a child—and how we might hear it in light of what the decision to follow Jesus is like: "A child came out of me. I cannot understand this, or try to explain it. Except to say that my past life has become foreign to me. Except to say that I am prey, for the rest of my life, to every small thing."[3]

Of course, the biggest of all small things—the child being born on the big day—was once, as we saw in chapter 1, an exceedingly small thing. The actual moment of conception? Yes, you had sex (or yes, you put in time and money at the fertility clinic). And yes, some couples are deliberately fastidious: she takes her temperature, he checks his watch after they are done. But the second penetration, not the one they both felt quite intensely, but the smaller, microscopic one of the sperm poking its way through the membrane and into the egg: unbeheld, unfelt, unmarked, this definitive moment when, as Siddhartha Mukherjee puts it, the genes from mom and dad "hug each other and readily swap genetic information."[4] Right then, already, the long roadmap of your life is fixed: gender, race, body type, hair and eye color, chances of disease, and so on.

It's well we don't ponder all this, or we'd try to rush in, shouting, "No!" "Wait!" "Yes!" "Oh my goodness!" We'd ponder imponderables like "Stars in their courses," "Fortune's wheel," or even "God's will." How do we picture God's engagement in that most telling of all moments? Does God the knitter, right then in your womb, knit together a new person (Ps. 139:13)? Or is it a more happenstance union of chromosomes and then—*Voila!*—you get the person you get?

News of the Pregnancy

How did the news of the pregnancy come? A private test at home? A doctor's verdict? God sent Gabriel to notify Mary. It's interesting that we speak of pregnancy "scares." This news might create consternation, panic, or terror. God can use the widest possible variety of responses to the news, including the most sober and even regretful. When we realized Lisa was pregnant, we experienced not just total shock but also an unanticipated regret. We just didn't feel ready.

Years later, we've joked that Sarah turned out to be the most loved, unwanted child in history.

A well-cultivated spiritual life will always harbor a kind of trembling uncertainty in the face of becoming a parent. Despite the shivers we felt, I can admit I thought parenting would be easier than it turned out to be. No one is capable of all that will be required. Karl Barth, a father of five, reminds us that parents are "just as weak and frail and fallible as their children. From a heavenly standpoint, they are indeed only older children."[5] The news of a pregnancy is humbling, as it should be, and it marks a time for living into dependence on God and community.

Back in the day we waited however long seemed to be the right amount of time to wait, or until we couldn't contain the news any longer, and then we started phoning people. I was listening in when Lisa called her mom. Lisa said, "Hi, Mom." And her mom immediately asked, "Are you pregnant?" Does the news travel by some mystical, clairvoyant umbilical cord between those formerly tied by a real umbilical cord? Nowadays the news is cleverly posted to Facebook or tweeted. Delight spreads. If evangelism is the spread of Good News, I wonder if the joyful dissemination of the word "She's pregnant" might shape our ability to share the news that God in Christ is coming into the world.

The news gradually ripples outward, and then you aren't just Jane or Jennifer any longer. You're pregnant. Meaghan O'Connell speaks of "the authority of the pregnant person."[6] People are concerned; they ask questions; they yield seats on the train; they volunteer to carry things for you. So much fuss can be exhausting. Angela Garbes voiced what her early pregnancy felt like—and she is not alone: "For a few weeks, that embryo the size of a pea felt like an unfathomably large black hole into which, at moments, my sanity was at risk of being sucked."[7]

The pregnant woman becomes the receptacle of other people's memories, sorrows, and anxieties. As if she's hung a "free counseling" sign over her belly, the pregnant woman hears stories, her simple presence a confessional booth for people to work out unresolved issues. Perhaps dimly they have the faintest recollection of being toted around inside their own moms.

Restraint and an excess of politeness are required. The pregnant woman's body gets treated as public property. I was flabbergasted by people, mere acquaintances and even strangers, who would actually reach out and lay a hand on Lisa's belly. Is it inappropriate weirdness? Or is it some visceral impulse to join physically to the wonder, perhaps to be blessed just a little by the priestly carriage of a woman who forgets she is carrying around in public the very life of God, which people yearn for so desperately?

Expecting Expectations

During pregnancy, parents try to do all the right things. Soon-to-be moms eat healthfully, limit alcohol and caffeine, and exercise. Many parents play music to the child in utero. I know a mom who played Mozart while her son was in her womb and then was disappointed that he didn't care for Mozart as an adolescent, although, truth be told, she didn't care for it herself.

All the simplistic advice with which the mom-to-be is peppered from books and well-wishers adds a lot of pressure, as if there's a right and a wrong way to do all sorts of things. What to expect while you're expecting? You can expect the expectations of other people, a piling on top of the weight you're already hauling around. The Christian, striving to do the right things during pregnancy, quite reflexively and happily realizes she just can't control these things, or anything else for that matter. Christians should be accustomed to confessing that we are not in control. We do not know how our story will unfold; all we know is that God will be there when we get there, and that will be enough.

This curious time of having less control over your life than usual, or of feeling entirely out of control, manifests itself in visible ways. There is the sheer awkwardness of inhabiting a body that doesn't behave as it has in the past. Anne Enright shares what she experienced: "I put on weight in odd places. I went to the kitchen in the middle of the night to see what nameless but really specific thing I was starving for. I sat down on the floor in front of the open fridge and cried."[8]

The simple reality that a pregnancy takes time, many weeks of time, is theologically interesting. We can ponder the spirituality that waiting is—in pregnancy and in all of life. "They who wait for the LORD shall renew their strength" (Isa. 40:31). That baby doesn't come right now or next week. You wait. And you continue to wait, often past the date the doctor pinpointed as your due date. We harried, busy, frenetic, impatient people are no good at waiting. Pregnancy can be a time to cultivate that sense of expectant waiting, of looking over a long time for the coming of God, for the hope God is delivering out on the horizon somewhere (Ps. 130:5).

During the waiting, various decisions are made. Which room will be the nursery? How will we decorate? Lisa's mom, as her first of countless acts of grandmotherly love, created a lovely stenciled pattern, which she then painted on the walls of what formerly had been our guest room. Lisa and I decided to take Lamaze classes. The teachers implied that moms who resorted to pain medications during delivery were wimpy; all should embrace "natural" childbirth. We studied, and we practiced the breathing—but when the time came and the first deadly serious contraction sent Lisa writhing, she wanted an epidural, and *Now!* As someone highly sensitive to pain, I wanted it urgently for her as well.

The Risk of Birth

Increasingly, many couples in America are choosing earthier, home-based approaches; midwifery is on the rise again, and doulas stay busy. All professionals who assist in birth endure the ultimate in on-call unpredictability and weird hours. Jennifer Worth, in her memoir that inspired the long-running television series *Call the Midwife*, ruminated on her arduous career of delivering babies and trying to save mothers in a poor neighborhood in London: "Why did I ever start this? I must have been mad. . . . Two-thirty in the morning. I struggle, half-asleep, into my uniform. Only three hours sleep after a seventeen-hour working day. Who would do such a job?"[9] Midwives, perhaps without realizing it, stand in the tradition of the Bible's first heroic civil disobedients, Shiphrah and Puah, who dissed the Pharaoh and deceptively allowed Hebrew boys to live (Exod. 2). When Jesus was born, didn't a local midwife from Bethlehem arrive to assist? What was her name? Tantalizingly, the Bible even employs the metaphor of God as midwife, the one delivering new life (Pss. 22:9; 71:6; Isa. 66:9).

Still, many (like us) suspect it's best to be in a hospital—just in case. Interactions with the medical institutions will figure prominently in the rest of life. A couple introduces their child into a lifelong relationship with medicine at the obstetrician's office and in a preliminary hospital visit. We took a tour of the labor and delivery facilities at Presbyterian Hospital, which were touted as the latest and greatest, more comfortable than home itself, as if you were securing a spa reservation at a seaside resort. I raised my hand and asked, "What if the labor and delivery rooms are full?" The facilitator chided me, saying, "They're never full."

Of course, you can see where this story is headed. On April 2, 1987, Lisa woke me up and asked me to time her contractions. Two minutes?! We scrambled into the car and dashed to the hospital. I dropped Lisa at the door, where someone was waiting with a wheelchair. After I parked the car, I came in the same door where I'd left her and inquired, "Where is Lisa Howell?" A nurse glanced at her clipboard, looked up, and said, "She's in the high risk area." I was immediately worried—but as it turned out, she was taken to high risk not because of any risk but because the labor and delivery rooms were full. Vindication. I was so happy—in an embarrassingly small-minded way.

And yet "high risk" is exactly where all life comes to be. So much can and does go wrong. Madeleine L'Engle described it flawlessly when she reflected on the birth of Jesus:

> This is no time for a child to be born,
> With the earth betrayed by war & hate . . .
> In a land in the crushing grip of Rome;
> Honour & truth were trampled by scorn—
> Yet here did the Saviour make his home.
>
> When is the time for love to be born?
> The inn is full on the planet earth,
> Yet Love still takes the risk of birth.[10]

Perhaps it is this mystical intersection between perilous risk and embracing hope that is what Courtney Martin describes as that "liminal space" just prior to giving birth:

> It fits all of life onto the head of a pin. No room for goals or shame
> or disappointment. There is just you, a very corporeal you, and this
> new human, trying (sometimes reluctantly) to become two, to survive,
> to make history. . . . You don't think about the laundry or the diapers
> or the pumping or the burping. You don't think about the moment,
> far into the future, when she'll surprise you to tears. . . . You don't
> think about the presidential election. You don't think about whether
> this was the best time to have a kid. It never is. Oh well. You don't
> think about the fact that 350,000 other women are also going to give
> birth on this day. . . . You don't think. You exist in a space and time
> without language. You, the consummate moderate, surrender to the
> extremes. You, the lover of words, realize there are none, really. You
> let your body take over. You trust it. You wait. Because you have no
> control, really. And you realize this is probably more true of the rest
> of life than you often pretend.[11]

Labor Pains

The time finally comes. Maybe. Is it labor or just Braxton Hicks? Is progress rapid or a snail's pace? I know women who've spent dozens of hours in labor. And I have a coworker who had twins who arrived so swiftly she and her husband never got out of their driveway.

Tina Cassidy described things humorously but with pristine accuracy: "Giving birth can make a perfectly dignified woman walk naked in front of strangers, threaten to murder her husband, or tell a nurse to stuff it. Women have tolerated unnatural labor positions, 'little snips,' humiliating enemas, unnecessary shavings, dangerous instruments, embarrassing hospital gowns. . . . They've been told to pant like dogs, deliver under water, bounce on balls, let doulas draw pretty pictures on their backs."[12] And much more. A frightening array of tools have been wielded over the centuries by doctors and midwives divining how best to get the baby out. The history of childbirth in civilized cultures makes you shudder. Women have been strapped to tables, handcuffed, and dehumanized in unspeakable ways. Methods have improved, and women have helped other women to retain their dignity through an undignified, if utterly beautiful, process.

Paul spoke glowingly about being a fool for Christ, and many Christians embrace that they may seem a laughingstock to the world. But for sheer physical humiliation, childbirth is hard to top or glamorize or spiritualize. It is moving, though, to overhear God's prophet Isaiah announcing to hopeless exiles that God is about to do a new thing. He uses these words:

> For a long time I have held my peace,
>   I have kept still and restrained myself;
> now I will cry out like a woman in labor,
>   I will gasp and pant. (Isa. 42:14 NRSV)

God as woman in labor. Could a laboring mother manage to remember this as she battles through the agonies?

And then there's the pain. God's most insensitive understatement in all of Scripture might be "I will greatly multiply your pain in childbearing" (Gen. 3:16). Women scramble for adjectives and pile on adverbs too when they try to explain how much it hurts. The bad theological salve Christians apply so vapidly to one another, "God doesn't give us more than we can bear," should not be attempted on a woman during an intense contraction (see fig. 6).

Having watched my wife in labor, deeply sympathetic but never having felt any such piercing pain myself, I can only share what others have shared. Rachel Marie Stone writes that "nothing can take away the pain. You can't fight the ocean, or tame its billows, and trying will only exhaust you. All there is to do is ride the waves and keep your head mostly above the water. It's like being sucked into a rip current: you'll die of exhaustion if you fight it, but you'll live if you swim alongside it, letting it carry you until you and it part ways."[13] Although they might be reticent to admit it, some women would prefer a C-section to hours of labor and having their flesh torn instead of surgically opened.

We Christians have it in our spiritual DNA to do our best to discern meaning and even beauty in suffering. In *Anna Karenina*, Kitty's cries

© Frank Chike Anigbo

FIGURE 6. *A Study for Agony and Ecstasy*, 2016, by Frank Chike Anigbo

from her labor shatter the heart of her husband, Levin. A tenderness in her gaze "told him not only that she did not reproach him but that she loved him for just this suffering." Levin continues, "If not I, then who is to blame for it? he thought involuntarily, seeking some culprit to punish for it; but there was no culprit. She suffered, she complained, and she triumphed in this suffering; she rejoiced in it and she loved it. He saw that something splendid was taking place in her soul, but what was it? He could not understand. It was too lofty for his comprehension."[14]

The intense, knee-buckling pain that is giving birth is barely endurable. Mark Sloan wisely points out that "childbirth is perhaps the only human condition in which pain is considered to be an unqualified good. It's also the only one in which the decision to reduce or eliminate pain is the subject of sometimes ferocious debate."[15] Nausea is reputed to be "good" if mom feels it during her first trimester; at no other time do people smile and say, "Oh good! You're nauseous!"

Redemptive Suffering

Paradoxically, the pain of childbirth is "good," perhaps in the way Good Friday is "good." Did Jesus understand this when he comforted his disciples, who perhaps had never felt or even witnessed this "good" pain up close, and who dreaded the implications of the crucifixion to come? "When a woman is in travail, she has sorrow, . . . but when she is delivered of the child, she no longer remembers the anguish, for joy that a child is born into the world" (John 16:21). A few days earlier, Jesus had prophesied the coming of wars and other apocalyptic horrors: "This is but the beginning of the birth-pangs" (Matt. 24:8).

These thoughts fit into one of the curious and persistent themes in Christianity: suffering isn't something we avoid but something we embrace and even seek. We may feel buffaloed when reading about medieval mystics who wore hair shirts and flagellated themselves as they pursued union with the agonies of Christ's suffering. But the biblical ennobling of suffering, even if alien to modern versions of a Christian life, is something for the serious Christian to ponder.[16] Jesus urges us to take up our crosses (Matt. 16:24). People in Jesus's day would have pictured somebody beaten and bloodied, carrying a wooden shaft onto which he would be nailed. Paul, whose thorn in the side was never removed, praised suffering as productive of endurance and hope (Rom. 5:4); and then, right after inviting us to imagine an infant, toddler-like relationship with God, whom we can call Abba as a wee one would, Paul speaks of us a "heirs of God"—"provided we suffer with him" (8:17).

Saint Francis of Assisi was so eager to be one with Christ that when he contemplated the crucifixion, he prayed to feel the ghastly pain Christ felt on the cross—a prayer God answered by inflicting the stigmata on Saint Francis's hands, feet, and side, which bled intermittently for the rest of his life. I wonder if his mother, Pica, was still alive to see this, perhaps even to comfort him from time to time in his pain. Did she shudder to see the lifeblood she'd given him seeping out of the hands she'd held? Far, far more modestly and less ambitiously, we fast during Lent, bearing a bit of misery in hopes of growing simultaneously into God and into the involuntary sufferings of the hungry and desolate among God's creatures. Do the contractions paving the way to birth set the stage for beneficial sufferings to come?

To any who mitigate labor pains as temporary and so very "worth it," I'd commend Lionel Shriver's novel *We Need to Talk about Kevin*, in which she narrates the savage eloquence of Eva: "So I made an effort, at which point I had to recognize that I'd been resisting the birth. Whenever the enormous mass approached that tiny canal, I'd been sucking it back. Because it hurt. It hurt a whole lot. In the New School course, they drummed into you that the pain was good, you were supposed to go with it, push into the pain, and only on my back did I contemplate what [terrible] advice this was. Pain, good? I was overcome with contempt."[17]

Whether listening to a woman in labor or trying to respond to any suffering on God's good earth, Christians must resist their habitual tendency to trivialize pain—as if the Gospel themes of redemption, hope, and eternal life somehow transform suffering into pleasure. Pain is. Jesus wasn't play-acting when he shrieked in agony that God, his Father, had utterly forsaken him on the cross. He was abandoned by those closest to him, who evidently couldn't bear to watch—although his mother stayed, watching the lifeblood she had given him drain out of him.

Who else was at the cross? Who is present for the birth? Contemporary culture often decides this: my dad was relegated to a waiting room, but if I had waited in a waiting room, I'd have been thought a cad. Historically, across many cultures, only women have been permitted into the birthing space. When the anthropologist Brigitte Jordan studied birth habits in the Yucatán, she discovered an exception: occasionally the husband would be briefly ushered into the delivery hut—to be sure he would see and understand just how much his bride was suffering![18] Evidently, back in 1522 a male German physician, eager to observe a birth, disguised himself as a woman, was caught doing so, and was burned at the stake.[19] In our culture, the dad is there, occasionally a mom or friend, and certainly doctors and nurses. But why?

Medicalized Patients

In my church there hangs a marvelous painting of the crucifixion by the Russian painter Geli Korzhev, which captures the moment on

Good Friday that may well have been the most harrowing and painful of all: when the soldiers, wielding hammers, were nailing Jesus to the cross. Jesus is flat on his back—a position exceedingly rare in the thousands of paintings of our Lord.

Lisa labored and tried her darnedest to give birth lying down. No one told us, or maybe no one knew, how very unusual, and even how unfortunate this is as the posture to assume in childbirth. Outside the United States, women sit or squat. Studies have shown that a more upright, seated or squatting position is not only more comfortable but also lessens pain and increases the strength of pushing—and the baby enjoys somewhat higher levels of oxygen through the umbilical cord during birth. So why do Americans, who fantasize that they are the greatest, lie down? The answer resides in the degree to which we have medicalized birth in America. Far more than any other society, we conceive of the laboring mom as a patient; she is admitted to a hospital to be treated by doctors and nurses.

Brigitte Jordan's studies of how different people in different cultures do what they do when it comes to childbirth are fascinating—and dumbfounding.[20] In the Yucatán, for instance, births take place at home, usually in a one-room house that is the house of the new mom's own mother, who's there to help. During pregnancy the midwife builds a solid relationship with the expectant mom, gauging her tolerance for pain and the strength of her family support. Massages are regular: the midwife treats the back and the belly of the mom, relaxing her, and keeping the baby turned. If the labor seems slow, the mom isn't given medicine but a raw egg—which causes her to vomit, producing pressure below on the baby.

But for those in the United States, medication is the norm. Jordan has recorded that women elsewhere use little to no pain medication. And thus, without pharmacology's involvement, moms are wide awake and alert immediately after birth, whereas many American women are groggy. I recall Lisa battling to stay awake and focused right after Noah's birth; it did not occur to me that the pain medications were inducing her sleepiness.

In the Yucatán, the mom begins her labor in a hammock and delivers right there, unless she moves to a chair. In either place, the dad or another loved one stands at her head over the hours, pushing back on her shoulders, energetically joining the mother in the arduous labor. The midwife is working hard physically too, still massaging. This shared labor is striking and lovely, reminding me of Paul's admonition to us to "bear one another's burdens, and so fulfil the law of Christ" (Gal. 6:2).

Jordan has also recorded noise differences between laboring women in the United States and in other countries. Jordan's studies suggest that women in the United States are louder—because the woman feels the need to express her intense level of pain in order to underline her need for medication. She wonders if the experience of pain is paradoxically heightened because of the ready availability of painkillers. Whereas if they simply aren't available, she wonders if the mother would not feel so much agony.[21]

Labor, in every place, takes time—and we might ponder what's called "non-progressing labor," which continues for hours, maybe days, all the pain apparently achieving nothing but sheer exhaustion. Lauren Winner asked if "non-progressing labor" is how God feels, "looking around our world; at our wars; at our heedless destruction of the environment; at the violence behind closed doors in every one of our neighborhoods. Is this what God feels when God looks at our daily small dishonesties and our envy? Is this what God feels when God sees my routine unkindnesses, my fears, my selfishness, my own failure to progress? Is God bone-tired?"[22]

Delivered of a Son

As the culmination of either days or minutes of labor, the baby finally arrives. When the Duchess of Cambridge, the former Kate Middleton, gave birth to a boy, Kensington Palace released the news: "Her Royal Highness The Duchess of Cambridge was safely delivered of a son."[23] *Delivered*: what a theologically robust word. Sometime as the Middle Ages segued into the Renaissance, this verb entered our language from a French word meaning "set free, liberate." The mother, indeed, is relieved of a heavy, ponderous burden. The postal worker delivers the mail. We speak of a baseball player delivering in the clutch. We speak of our deliverance from sin and death—and the childbirth analogy reminds us that it's not merely that I get saved; there is new life beyond just me.

A woman who's just pushed out something so little that feels so huge wouldn't want to thumb through a science textbook. But she might fall on her knees in immense gratitude to know that the evolution of the size of the brain is delicately related to the ability to walk on two feet. Should the human brain evolve any larger, the ability of the hips to balance on two feet, which requires a fairly narrow pelvis, would be compromised. Awful as delivery might be, a more highly evolved brain and thus head size would worsen the ordeal beyond bearing.

What other human experience connects terrible pain and sheer joy so tightly? The range of emotions for women who have just delivered is as wide as the world. Some report "I'm so in love!" while others are just relieved it's over. Mary Costello, in her novel *Academy Street*, describes the unfolding moments of delivery. "The pain struck at dawn. . . . In the hospital foyer her waters broke. She looked down at her drenched shoes and began to cry. That evening when it was all over she thought she had scaled Everest, stood at its peak, exhilarated. The next morning the enormity of it all hit her. She had brought forth life, rendered human something from almost nothing, and this power, this ability to create, overwhelmed her."[24] I wonder sometimes if God vouchsafes this sort of daunting, painful, overwhelming experience to us so we might get some slight glimpse into the heart of God—and how God felt in creating everything from nothing at all, how God feels in continuing to bring forth life, and what the New Creation might be like. Not so much for us, but for God. Though not often acknowledged, someone endured striking pain and tears so that I, the writer, and you, the reader just now, might simply be. And God was there, feeling it all, loving, agonizing, celebrating.

Oddly enough, the labor isn't quite done. The placenta is waiting in line to be delivered. This lifeline, this sac of nourishment that has carried more than one-fifth of mom's blood for weeks now, has to come out. Although hospitals dispose of the thing quickly and out of sight, it does seem sacred in some way. Many primates, also some human beings, actually eat the thing. In some cultures it is buried in the ground as a promise of fertility and good crops. Pawnee midwives wrap it in leather and hang it up in a tree, believing this will ease the difficulty of the next birth; or it's buried deep underground if the woman wants no more children.[25]

For the parents and for the obstetrician, nurse, or midwife, the birth is a birth only after the obligatory checking of things, counting fingers and toes, and, of course, hearing the first cry. Meaghan O'Connell describes it beautifully: "And then I heard a cry. This isn't possible, it's an incorrect feeling, if feelings can be described as incorrect, but what I felt above all at that moment was recognition. Hearing his cry was like seeing a familiar face in a crowd. I was lying on my back staring at the ceiling, shaking, tears streaming down my cheeks. His cry, I was surprised to find, sounded like him. He sounded like his own person. Before that moment, all baby cries had sounded the same to me, but his cry was a voice. A self."[26]

NINE

The First Days after Birth

For most American families, birth happens in a hospital, which is where those mind-boggling first moments of life unfold. In some other civilizations, the same magic happens at home. But in every place, except when the newborn is under extreme duress, after a couple of days the new family claws its way toward normalcy—the "new normal," in which nothing is ever the same.

Our firstborn arrived by C-section, so we got the padding of a couple of additional days in the hospital. I recall thinking, "This is a piece of cake," underestimating the value of nurses and aides, baby professionals who were popping in and out regularly, advising, and assisting. Our first child, Sarah, mostly slept anyhow; she seemed so peaceful—what I guess they call "an easy baby." I did not know at the time that the medications they had injected into Lisa for the surgery also left our daughter a little bit on the sluggish side.

Until it was time to go home. We gathered up our prizes—all the flowers, cards, and stuffed animals. A candy striper pushed Lisa in a wheelchair with Sarah in her lap to the elevator and then to the car, right by the front door. We piled everything into the cute little Subaru station wagon we'd purchased, struggling a bit to figure out the straps and buckles of the infant car seat. And then the candy striper said goodbye and closed the door.

As if on cue, Sarah let out an ungodly howl, or I should say howls, a stunningly impressive and depressing sequence of screams, sobs, and heavings. Instead of turning out into Hawthorne Lane toward home, I circled back to the front door of the hospital, but the candy striper was gone. "Something's wrong. Can we take her back?" Lisa looked as shaken as I felt—and we knew it was just the two of us now. Or rather, the three of us.

I can only assume that all parents have this "Oh my good Lord God Almighty" moment when they feel the crushing weight of the responsibility of this fragile life entrusted to such untutored amateurs. Yes, we'd read books and sat through classes. But nothing prepares you for the constant pressure of problem-solving, guessing what this cry or that cry might mean, and making so many mistakes. I stuck the diaper safety pin into Sarah's hip. I lifted her above my head playfully and jammed her head into the door frame. The first time I was flat-out positive something was wrong with her, I strapped her into the car seat and drove quickly to the pediatrician's office. She was fine. The nurses restrained their chuckles as they sent us right back home.

May the Force Be with You

And yet, as a pastor, I've seen children rushed off to open heart surgery during week one. I've sat with parents numb from watching their baby fighting for its life. These wee ones are so very wee, so tiny, so fragile. Once upon a time you were so very vulnerable as well. If you have children, you have good cause to fret over them.

And it's a tough world out there. The smartest, most prepared and loving parents struggle and can wind up riddled with the peculiar humiliation only a parent can feel. It's the foolish parent who thinks, "I've got this," as if it's a matter of skill, knowledge, and savvy. Sam Wells was right: "The parent who seeks the credit or claims compensatory acknowledgment for their labors or infant-management is missing the bigger part of the deal: some force is acting in, through, and with the growing child—a force with its own momentum, own wisdom, own creativity, pace, dynamic and character; such that any parent that seeks to control, bridle, or harness it is a prisoner of their own fears and a fool in their own hubris."[1]

When the candy striper said goodbye, she should have added, "May the Force be with you." At every stage, but especially in those earliest hours and days of a child's life, parents need God. After all, God made you and this child and the world in which breathing and sustenance and gravity and grace all happen. God is active in you and your child, whether you realize it or not. God is just as active, caring, and totally engaged in the children of cynics, doubters, and outright atheists, and in the children of people who puzzle, mortify, or frighten you. When Jesus taught us to pray, he suggested we begin with "our Father," not "my Father." The "our" isn't just the people in our closest circle or those who know and love Jesus. God is our Father, Father to all of us and to those different from us too.

God is just as much (or maybe more?) our Mother. We need a father and a mother both, and both bring rich blessings to us. Some of us get one or the other, and even the best mothers and fathers aren't always the blessings they might be to their children. For me, one of the most poignant and provocative thoughts about Mary and mothers and Jesus comes from the pen of the medieval mystic Julian of Norwich. Her visions of Jesus pulsate with powerful love and tender comfort—and no passage moves me as much as when Julian explains that "Jesus Christ is our true Mother." "We have our being from him. . . . Our true Mother Jesus bears us for joy. . . . He carries us within him in love and travail." Jesus our Mother "feeds us with his own self."[2]

Consider that astonishing promise of hope God made in Isaiah 49:15–16 (in John Goldingay's translation):

> Can a woman put her baby out of mind,
>   so as not to have compassion on the child of her womb?
> Yes, these may put out of mind,
>   but I—I cannot put you out of mind.
> There, on my palms I have engraved you.[3]

How special are you? How special is each child? God our Mother holds us always in her strong hands.

Attachment and Attunement

What I didn't appreciate as we drove away from the hospital was that a profound bond had already been established between us and our newborn. Psychologists can explain the detailed dynamics of what parents have engaged in intuitively since the first human-ish people bore children. In the first moments of life, and continuing through the first days and then weeks, a deep, powerful bond is formed with one's parents. We may call what unfolds *attachment theory*: a child wants and needs to become attached to a very specific, consistently present, and nurturing face (or to a small number of faces); to learn and require the particular feel of her arms and his rocking; to feel the immense and reassuring comfort in this regular attention. Once words begin to resonate in the infant's mind, this is called love. When there is hunger, pain, or discomfort of any kind, these people come running. They are always there.

Beyond this blanket of security that is the nursery and the home, infants need what has been called "joyful dialogic companionship"[4] with their parents. These emotional interactions are pivotal in the development of the brain and the self. At this point, attachment is well in place. Now an "attunement" goes on between parent and child. Through exchanged emotional encounters, they get in sync, and the child begins to experience a rhythm of mood and expression, and the child draws permanent conclusions, such as, "I am understood" or "I belong" or "I am beloved" or "I get on his nerves" or any number of messages. It's not one way, the parents pouring immense love into the hollow vessel of the child. From the outset, there is reciprocity. An infant perceives truly that she has an impact on dad. A baby boy squints, turns up a corner of his mouth, and mom replies with a similar gesture or a coo.

This "joyful dialogic companionship," this "attunement," is remarkably like prayer—or at least what prayer could be. We are simply with God. The mutual need just to be together is immense. Meaghan O'Connell was surprised that, in her first encounter with her son after birth, "he knew better than I did what to do. My job was to just be still, to look at him with admiration, to let relief wash over me—the relief of being met, finally, halfway. He sucked and sucked, needing me like no one ever had before."[5] We need God. God needs us. Ours is to be still.

Breastfeeding

Breastfeeding is another challenging aspect of a baby's first days. For some it's a breeze, for others a daunting struggle, tinged with feelings of guilt. Considerable mystique around the benefits of breast milk adds to the pressure. The ancient Greeks even believed that the Milky Way resulted from a spill while Hera was breastfeeding Hercules; each droplet in the splattering became a speck of light.[6] Quite a stretch for something so "normal": we are among millions of mammals who produce milk.

Anne Enright offers a humorous portrayal of the experience for the mom:

> What fun! to be granted a new bodily function so late in life. As if you woke up one morning and could play the piano. . . . It is quite pleasant when a part of your body makes sense after many years. . . . You feed your child, it seems, on hope alone. There is nothing to see. You do not believe the milk exists until she throws it back up, and when she does, you want to cry. What is not quite yours as it leaves you, is definitely yours as it comes back.[7]

As we've seen, the newborn, quite innately knows where to go searching for nourishment. This primal intimacy isn't passive on either side. Mom and child are in a surprisingly dialogical relationship. Yes, the child receives, but so does mom—as Angela Garbes points out: "The nutritional and immunological components of breast milk change every day, according to the specific, individual needs of the baby."[8] It's the baby's backwash that signals to the mother's breast about what the baby needs. And the baby helps the mom to heal: when the baby licks or sucks the nipple, a hormone (oxytocin) is released into her bloodstream, which helps to contract the uterus and reduces bleeding so the mother returns to well-being.[9]

Since God came to us as an infant, might we see in the infant's ineluctable desire for the breast the Lord's desire for us? Medieval mystics playfully spoke of the Bible's two testaments as two breasts on which we feed—and that each mother, when nursing, is one with Mary in her feeding of her infant son. As the Greeks saw breast milk in the sky, and as the Egyptians depicted the goddess Isis as breast-feeding the Pharaoh, so Christians have expanded on the image in Isaiah 49 of God as nursing mother. Saint Bernard of Clairvaux, among countless medieval theologians, envisioned God's holy breasts from which flow to us grace and mercy.[10]

Waiting on Words

Very early in life, infants begin recognizing and eventually under-standing words. Eventually, the child speaks. What fun it would be if the child would pop out of the womb, look up at you and say, "Hi! Mom? Brrr. . . . It's cold in here. Can I eat now?" Thankfully, they cannot. This is of special interest theologically. Waiting on words requires some patience and tenderness. Anything that requires us to wait, whether we're waiting for the child to be born or waiting for them to utter a first word or sentence, can be a healthy spiritual discipline for those of us in a culture so focused on instant gratifica-tion and staying busy. What if, while waiting for an infant to finally speak, a parent pondered these words? "For God alone my soul waits in silence" (Ps. 62:1). "My soul waits for the LORD, more than watch-men for the morning" (Ps. 130:6). "They who wait for the LORD shall renew their strength" (Isa. 40:31).

Why children can't speak is fascinating. At some moment in evolu-tionary time, the Cro-Magnon people (famous for their cave paintings in Lascaux, France, and Altamira, Spain) became the first hominids who could choke on food. Not a happy development—except it was identical to the development that made speech possible. The larynx descended far enough to enable speech—and choking. For an infant, in God's good mercy, the larynx has not yet descended at birth, so children do not generally choke. When they are a bit older, choking can happen, but then so can speech. How lovely they come out with-out words and survive, but then talk later on when they are better equipped not to choke. Wenda Trevathan is right: "Language has contributed far more to survival and success of humans than would the ability to swallow and breathe at the same time."[11]

From day one, and then increasingly as my children neared the magical moment of speech, I repeated to each of them, constantly and patiently, the word *Dada*, and then the sentence "I love Dada the most." None of them took this bait; they said other things—although Sarah's first real sentence, with a subject and a verb, did involve me. She looked out the window one day and said, "Dada mow." What were Jesus's first words? We can be sure that among his first words was the utterly simple *Abba*, much like our *Dada*. That's the name he would have used for Joseph, and then the name he boldly spoke when he prayed.

I do not know if children simply and directly learn speech from mom and dad or if Noam Chomsky was right and certain ground rules of language are innate. We do know that an infant prefers speech-like sounds over other sounds. And it doesn't matter which language is being spoken. All languages are learned and mastered at precisely the same pace. We've always heard how easy learning languages is for little ones, who can successfully figure out and use two structurally different languages simultaneously, like Chinese and English, with no textbooks or instructors—and they never confuse or blend them inappropriately.

Watching or recalling the way a child learns to talk might help us pray. Dietrich Bonhoeffer, as clouds of evil gathered over Europe in 1939, described how learning to pray is like learning to talk: "The child learns to speak because his father speaks to him. He learns the speech of his father."[12] We pray early, often, and audibly, so our child will learn how to speak with God. We might wonder if the remarkable gift of communication is what being made in God's image is all about.

We even begin to read God's words to an infant early in life. Maryanne Wolf reminds us that decades of research shows that "the amount of time a child spends listening to parents and other loved ones read is a good predictor of the level of reading attained years later." And why? "The child can learn to associate the act of reading with a sense of being loved."[13] Reading is love. Reading together is love. Reading God's Word is love. God's Word is love.

Waking Up to the World

Of course, immediately after birth, parents become attentive to various aspects of physical development. The brain, interestingly enough, doesn't grow the way we'd imagine. The number of brain cells in a child and in an adult are about the same. It's the connections that literally blow your mind. In the infant's young brain, as many as two million new connections—we call them synapses—are formed every second. You'd expect smoke to rise from their scalps or the lights in the delivery room to flicker. By age two a child has over one hundred trillion such synapses, double what an adult has! But then the brain begins to shed thousands and millions of them, based on environment, what's needed, what isn't. The maturing brain has fewer, but strong, connections.[14] Early experiences of love, grace, mercy, justice, community, and even holiness strengthen synapses, and the Christian life literally feels more natural than if those connections strike the child as useless or unneeded.

Luckily, the child's skull is soft, malleable, even open a little, allowing for rapid growth and adjustment. An infant is not hard-headed!—or at least not yet. We may covet their malleable skulls and their lack of hardheadedness, and ponder how making new mental connections and shedding old ones is actually a physiological possibility and a delight.

In those halcyon days shortly after birth, parents are determined to remember everything. You don't imagine you'll forget a single thing. But you do. For my generation, the baby book was our first helper—and we still relish thumbing through and reminiscing. Sure, you can shoot miles of video and record funny and special moments. But you still forget most of the precious content of a simple day at four days old or at three weeks or at seven months or at five years. All memory, of every beloved or cursed or joyful or sorrowful moment, is fully recalled in the mind of God—and I suspect that one of the unspeakably gleeful aspects of life in heaven is that God will download all that we have forgotten into our minds and souls, and we will then be able to fill those unending days with an overflow of gratitude and awe.

The infant cannot see far. As if by flawless divine design, the newborn can see just far enough to meet mom's eyes and to find her breasts. But that scope of vision is widening rapidly—and the young one must be dumbfounded by seeing each new thing. Imagine: children for the first time seeing a dog, a tree, a cloud, a mountain, a lake. No wonder that when they figure out how to talk, they never stop asking questions.

Annie Dillard ponders how children at some point wake up and "discover themselves to have been here all along." She wonders, "Is this sad? They wake like sleepwalkers, in full stride . . . surrounded by familiar people and objects, equipped with a hundred skills. . . . I woke in bits, like all children, piecemeal over the years. I discovered myself and the world. . . . Consciousness converges with the child as a landing tern touches the outspread feet of its shadow on the sand. . . . Like any child, I slide into myself perfectly fitted, as a diver meets her reflection in a pool."[15] In the earliest minutes after birth, parents get to be co-hosts, observers, and docents for the child's gradual and marvelous awakening to the world.

But not for all that long. No new parent can see it coming, but the parting begins the moment your son or daughter exits their dwelling inside mom, and the cord is cut. Kimberly Harrington reminds us of job number one in the parent's job description: "The primary purpose of this position is to train the people you love most in this world to leave you. Forever."[16] Dar Williams wrote an achingly beautiful song for her young daughter, anticipating her eventual parting.

> You'll fly away, but take my hand until that day.
> So when they ask how far love goes,
> When my job's done you'll be the one who knows.[17]

And when they eventually leave, you won't have gotten a long, complicated list of visions accomplished, but really just one or maybe two that are really one: our love and God's love. We could say our job as parents is for our children to know not just our love but God's love. But how else does God's love come to a newborn than through the ones they learn to call Mother and Father?

God's love blesses a child through the parents, midwives, doctors and nurses, neighbors, aunts, uncles, grandparents, and, of course, the church. It takes a village? It takes a church, and not just a nice place with a cute nursery and a preschool and neat children's programs. We need a church with companions who will be the Body of Christ for the child and parents, who will look for and see God in their faces. Winston Churchill, who thought all babies looked like him, got his first glimpse of the baby girl who would grow up to be Queen Elizabeth; he claimed to detect "an air of authority and reflectiveness astonishing in an infant."[18] Church people see some royalty in a newborn, the veritable image of God, a little temple of the Holy Spirit.

Dreams for the Newborn

Church helps us know how to dream. Perhaps the most important theological question to be asked at the birth of a child is, "What is God's dream for this child?" Parents have their own dreams. Often, these are not thought through but just what they've soaked up from their culture. I dream my child will be happy, healthy, and educated, and will climb a little higher on the ladder of success than I've managed. Ivy League education maybe? Challenge soccer status?

Wiser parents might aim a bit lower—or should we say higher? I might dream that my child's final words, at the end of a long life, might echo those of Gerard Manley Hopkins, "I am so happy. I am so happy. I loved my life,"[19] or of Raymond Carver, who says that he got what he wanted from his life:

> To call myself beloved, to feel myself
> beloved on the earth.[20]

God's dream overlaps with this sort of thing, and yet is pretty different. God dreams that each child will come to know and love God. God's dream can handle, embrace, and even delight in what might devastate or disappoint parental dreams. What we rank as a disability does not make God sigh with disappointment. Any time anyone anywhere for any reason is unwelcomed, God's heart is grieved. God weaves God's own image into all fetal life.

Midwife Jennifer Worth, whose memoir inspired the long-running television series *Call the Midwife*, tells the story of a white man whose white wife gave birth to a black child. When he saw the baby and realized he could not possibly be the father, after only the slightest pause, he said, "Well, I don't reckon to know much about babies, but I can see as how this is the most beautiful in the world."[21] God wouldn't have paused.

Earlier, we spoke of a child born with no limbs. The parents were mortified and rejected their own child, but the nurse adopted her and called her "the best Gift *ever*."[22]

God sees in every child the greatest kid ever. God's dream is that we will live into God's love and holiness. God's dream is that we will see God as God is—and then be moved and shaped always to see as God sees, to love as God loves. And to love those whom God loves.

The world has its own dreams for kids. At birth, God has a dream for each child: the dream of faith, living into the grace that birth actually is, and playing a part in God's dream for all the other children. It's tough out there, as the most beloved and the most disregarded wee ones suffer challenges that follow them for life. Mounting evidence has proven that Adverse Childhood Experiences (ACEs; negative experiences that happen around children in the earliest days of their lives), including trauma, neglect, violence, eviction from a home, alcoholism, chronic arguing, toxic stress and anxiety, can all put the child at much higher risk for a lifetime of health, social, and learning problems, not to mention heart disease, cancer, depression, divorce, alcoholism, and much more. Children whose cries go unanswered learn not to cry. Children who are not held often develop "indiscriminate friendliness," the tendency to smile and warm up to any and everybody, which looks so cute on the surface—but it's a coping strategy of neglected children.[23] As Donna Jackson Nakazawa puts it, "Your emotional biography becomes your physical biology"[24]— and the two then collaborate to write the script for the rest of your, or your child's, life.

Perhaps now we can see why many seemingly little things in an infant's earliest days aren't so little. If we think back, in light of these studies, to our own early childhood, can we make some sense of our own health, depression, anxiety, and other struggles? Hope and healing can come in many forms: through prayer, of course, but not through prayer alone. We can seek professional counseling, other kinds of therapy, and medical treatment to help us live into the curiously tough resilience we seem to be born with. Then all of us as God's people can work to change the kind of society in which we live: we clearly have a lot of work to do to realize God's dream.

TEN

Infertility and Medicine

It is impossible, and maybe even hard-hearted, to think very long about birth without pondering those times when a pregnancy is lost or when pregnancy never happens at all. In the next chapter, we will shudder as we reflect on miscarriage, stillbirth, and death of the newborn or the mother. And in this chapter we'll discuss difficulties surrounding becoming pregnant. Life, from conception onward, is always fragile. I barely made it; I might not have made it—and the same holds for you.

Infertility: Let's have a child! Hmm, not this month. We'll try again. And again. People keep asking when we're going to have children. If they only knew. The escalation of anxiety. An inexplicable but palpable sense of failure. Successful, type-A, can-do people confronted by an unexpected *can't*. Infertility is often unexpected. When we talk about pregnancy and birth, we often speak of expecting: "She's expecting a child" or "What to do when you're expecting." We never expected to be *not* expecting. In infertility our expectations, dreams, and fantasies that were once firmly implanted are now desperately out of reach.

Elizabeth Hagan's lovely memoir *Birthed: Finding Grace through Infertility* traces her story, which is the story of so many. Her "one big dream" was frustrated. Month by month, trying but then having another period. What did she feel as the bleeding began—again? She writes, "Devastation bled through me."[1] Well-meaning friends would inquire, "Why don't you just adopt?" as if this had never crossed her mind. Once more, earnest Christians hushing the voice of pain. After engaging professional birth specialists, Hagan reports, "My body became an object to be poked, prodded, and manipulated. At home, my body belonged to well-timed sex whether I was in the mood or not. Then, at some point during the month, my body bore the shame of a period. In all of these things, I hated my body."[2] Her overriding gut feeling, all her well-imbibed theology notwithstanding, was, "I felt as if God really hated me."[3]

We can be sure that church not only fails to help those who battle (and it feels like a battle) infertility. The church also unwittingly or thoughtlessly inflicts pain. At my church, many people walk in pushing strollers, looking stressed, and even complaining about how exhausted they are, not realizing the hollow exhaustion of the friend who'd give anything for the opportunity to push a stroller around. We have baptisms many Sundays. As I carry the cute infant down the aisle, while most people are oohing and aahing, I inevitably notice a young woman forcing a smile but with some barely hidden longing and pain just behind her eyes.

The Cruelty of the Church

Some churches are downright cruel. It's Mother's Day—and the tradition is to recognize the newest mother and the mother with the most children or to hand carnations to each mother as she enters the sanctuary. The carnation is extended by a grinning person. "Oh . . . what? You're not a mom?" Carnation withdrawn. Hospitality annihilated. Christ's Body suffers yet another piercing.

Comments are made such as, "Keep trying. We'll pray for you." "Just have a positive attitude!" "Trust God!" Or, in a different vein, parents speak in a rightly curious way of being "blessed" by having a child or by having a healthy child. But we say this in earshot of someone who is pursuing that very blessing so valiantly. Can we find ways to speak of God's gift of children in a way that doesn't isolate or crush others but actually embraces them?

The Bible has inflicted much harm when it comes to infertility. The barren woman gets much attention in Scripture, and it's often hopeful: "God remembered Rachel . . . and opened her womb" (Gen. 30:22); even the aged Sarah and Elizabeth conceived miraculously. And yet, most clearly, the gaping nothingness in the womb is chalked up to God. Of Hannah it is written that "the LORD had closed her womb" (1 Sam. 1:5); "the LORD had closed all the wombs of the house of Abimelech" (Gen. 20:18); and Jacob angrily reprimanded Rachel, for God "has withheld from you the fruit of the womb" (Gen. 30:2).

I might be wrong in the way I handle these passages. But I hope not, and if I am, I'll have quite a few questions for God when and if I get to heaven. Why would you "open" the womb of the victim of rape but not the holy and prayerful married woman? How exactly did you close a given womb? When the woman was in her own mother's womb, did you reach down and narrow her fallopian tubes? Or did you select a mate for her with a negligible sperm count?

Here's how the Bible works whether we're examining infertility or so-called holy war or natural disasters. The Bible's authors, who crafted its stories and passed down their fledgling and impressive faith to us, saw their lives as so hinged to God that they couldn't conceive of anything happening that wasn't directly from God's hand. And so they over-interpreted situations like infertility or storms or wars. Unable to picture anything apart from God, they assumed infertility was from God, that God tossed down thunderbolts, that God willed slaughter on the battlefield.

And yet, just as the true God we know from the rest of Scripture would never order genocide or hurl lightning down to slaughter hundreds of well-intended Canaanite prophets, God does not close wombs. Mind you, it's in the Bible. Rowan Williams described the Bible, with its peculiar, varied, and problematical contents flawlessly: "This is what God wants you to hear. . . . God is saying 'This is how people heard me, saw me, responded to me, this is the gift I gave them, this is the response they made. . . . We do not have to work on the assumption that God *likes* those responses."[4]

Why does infertility happen? Never, ever venture into that vaguely pious "Everything happens for a reason" zone. We know precisely

why infertility happens. Ask your OB/GYN or a reproductive endocrinologist. Wombs don't "open" because of quirks in ovulation,
the shape of reproductive organs, endometriosis, low sperm count,
the patency of the fallopian tubes, and many other factors. It's not the
woman's "fault," as society has believed for centuries. Catherine de
Medici was blamed for childlessness, even though everyone at court
knew Henry II had a malformed penis and was generally uninterested
in being amorous.

Shouldn't God at least help? How many millions of prayers have
been lifted up to Saint Anne, Jesus's grandmother and the patron saint
of the infertile? In the Middle Ages, women (realizing their worth
depended on bearing children, especially sons) turned to healers and
magic, went on pilgrimages, bought potions and amulets—all to no
avail.

In Vitro Fertilization

In modern times, at least in the world's wealthier cultures, God has
some helpers: reproductive endocrinologists. Mercifully, science has
advanced to the point that tests can discern the physical causes of
infertility. And science, for more than a generation now, can bypass
the time-honored way for people to become pregnant (or from the
child's perspective, to be conceived) by in vitro fertilization (IVF; *in
vitro* meaning "in glass"). Sperm and egg are joined in a dish outside
the body. In 1978, a news flash shocked the world: after her parents
had tried to conceive naturally for nine years and made no progress
(the would-be mom's fallopian tubes were blocked), Louise Brown
was born in the United Kingdom, the first human ever to have been
born as a result of IVF.

A firestorm of ethical controversy began. The Roman Catholic
Church, ever vigilant in matters of sexuality and reproduction, immediately and not surprisingly issued *Donum Vitae* in 1987 and *Dignitas
Personae* in 2008, both declaring that life created outside the bonds
of marriage was illicit. Various non-Vatican theologians have been
reticent to embrace the do-anything approach. Gilbert Meilaender,
noting that the "illness" being treated in reproductive endocrinology

is "the parents' desire for a child," suggests that "without in any way undervaluing the presence of children, we should also be free of the idolatrous desire to have them at any cost—as our project rather than God's gift."[5] Allen Verhey offered this indisputable theological wisdom: "Children are not the hope of the world and not the hope of a person's or a couple's flourishing. The child on whom the world's hope—and theirs—depends has been born."[6] Of course, we might recall that Jesus came to be in Mary's womb far outside the norm of a married couple's conjugal relations.

More positively, the "let nature take its course" stance is one we violate everywhere else. We treat closed bronchial tubes and infected urinary tracts, and we transplant kidneys and hearts; in a bone marrow transplant, we remove stem cells and freeze them for a time and then return them to the body. Who could ponder medicine and not be grateful for even simple medical advances, like antibiotics, which have saved tens of thousands of lives in childbirth?

A reproductive endocrinologist I visited rather adamantly insisted that he does not "transplant" an embryo into the uterus; he "transfers" the embryo. There is still some adjoining that may or may not occur, some magic that will then happen naturally or not—a little miracle, if you will. Could we see God watching over, caring about, superintending this process, or at least rooting for and with us? A theologian or an ethicist might argue against IVF. But how would anyone say to Louise Brown that she should not have come to be in 1978? She grew up and gave birth herself, after entirely natural conception, to two children (see fig. 7). Should they not exist either?

I've baptized dozens of children who made it into the world and then to the font because of medical technology. Recently, I confirmed twins who were born eighteen months after their mother had a hysterectomy. She had begun the IVF process, eggs already harvested, when her cancer was discovered. A surrogate carried her children to term.

Of course, even the finest medical procedures cannot guarantee a pregnancy. This hard truth comes as a shock to modern people in advanced cultures, as we have seized on an outsized faith in the ability of medicine to fix anything and everything. James Joel Shuman

FIGURE 7. Louise Brown, the world's first test-tube baby, sits with her children (Cameron, six, and Aiden, fifteen weeks) at the Bourn Hall Clinic in Cambridgeshire.

says, "When medicine falls short of the increasingly unrealistic expectations placed upon it by contemporary culture, that culture's significant and ever-increasing faith in science as a savior is typically not considered as a possible cause of the disappointment."[7]

Moral Quandaries

Medicine's track record is one to brag about. Medicine takes strides forward all the time, which introduces more dizzying dilemmas for people facing infertility. It is one thing to ask a doctor, "Can you help us have a child?" It is quite another to ask, "Can you help us have a particular kind of child?" Henry VIII didn't want a child; he wanted a son. When combined with genetic testing, IVF poses an endless array of ever-unfolding ethical quandaries—not to mention what happens when a lot of money is thrown into the mix. "We want a boy. We want a healthy boy. We want a healthy, smart boy. And blond." We may rightly feel we are walking down a hallway toward some Brave New World.

The technology and related legal tussles are so new that we find ourselves in uncharted waters. How will it all pan out? In a probably made-up old story, Marilyn Monroe told Albert Einstein she would love to have his baby: "With my looks and your brain, our child would be a gift to the world." Einstein wryly responded, "But my dear, what if the child had my looks and your brain?"[8] Can we manufacture a beautiful, blond-haired, blue-eyed genius with a fabulous physique?

Novelists are finding this dark pathway to be fertile ground. Nancy Kress, in her novella *Beggars in Spain*, imagines the unintended and nightmarish consequences of something as small as a genetic fix that would enable your child never to need sleep. The parents, quite sure that the extra hours will be a massive advantage over "normal" kids, never anticipate the unfolding horrors for their superior children—and everyone else.

Even the less ambitious face daunting enigmas. With embryo donors, surrogates who will carry someone else's embryo, sperm donors, and "reproductive tourism" (in which you travel to the state or country that will deliver what you need), how are we re-envisioning the gift of life? Our questions would have dumbfounded Jeremiah, Simon Peter, Thomas Aquinas, Teresa of Ávila, or Dorothy Day.

Our heads spun in 1986 when we read that Baby M was born to Mary Beth Whitehead, the woman who had contracted with the Stern family to carry their child, changed her mind and sued for the child, who then was awarded by the court to the Sterns. Who is the mother? The bearer? The raiser? The possessor of the ovum? As Meilaender points out, "We find ourselves trying to decide which of these 'functions' gives a woman most claim to be the mother. The very fact that surrogacy leads us into such conundrums may itself be good enough reason to turn against it."[9] But what about Baby M? Melissa Stern, twenty years old and a student at George Washington University, said this of William and Elizabeth Stern: "I'm very happy I ended up with them. I love them; they're my best friends in the whole world, and that's all I have to say about it."[10]

If we ask "What about Baby M?" we perhaps could also ask about the additional eggs that never wound up growing in anybody's womb. Many parents, after going through IVF, have shared with me a gnawing sense of uncertainty regarding the unused, unneeded embryos—quite often telling me, "We feel like we're playing God." Parents aren't the only ones baffled by embryos lying around. What is the liability for those who store them? Do they keep them for some period of time? Frozen embryos have been damaged at several clinics due to the failure of liquid nitrogen storage tanks.[11]

The courts have gotten tied up with many divorce cases that involve wrangling over who gets the frozen embryos, not to mention who can or can't use them and how. And then, post-birth, the expansion of the number of people involved in a birth (husband, wife, donor, surrogate) has given rise to ferocious and complicated custody disputes. During the presidencies of George W. Bush and Barack Obama, a national debate raged over whether unused embryos could find their place in stem-cell research.

Sprinting into an Abyss

Given the costs of procedures like IVF, we should ask who has access and who doesn't. Insurance scenarios changed when the American Society for Reproductive Medicine designated infertility as a "disease." Given my theological lean toward egalitarianism, I wonder how lingering infertility plays out for the rich versus for the poor. What about God's children in developing countries? With the widespread acceptance of same-gender marriage, many children are now born into families with two moms or two dads.

And, of course, alongside human brilliance is the nagging inevitability of human error. Indeed, as legal scholar Susan Crockin puts it, "'Reproductive wrongs' will take their place beside 'reproductive rights.'"[12] In 2002, a white couple in England gave birth to black twins. *Surprise!* Or we should say, *Surprise, Surprise!* Both the white couple and the black couple who made the original donation fought for custody of these twins.[13] Talk about a dramatic birth story to tell one day when you're grown.

When my parents had me, they wanted a boy, but they had no clues regarding my gender (beyond old wives' tales) until I popped out in the delivery room. Now parents can find out not only the gender but also much about the genetic makeup of the forthcoming child—and hence information about possible deficits, proclivity to diseases, and more. It is not hard to fathom why medical clinics that provide genetic testing also provide genetic counseling. What will you as parents do with whatever information surfaces? How will you determine whether the life within is worth living? I have sat with adamantly pro-life couples who have learned that the child growing in the womb isn't growing enough; a serious genetic disorder will most assuredly end the life of the child soon, perhaps in utero or perhaps hours after birth; the child will have a short life accompanied by agonizing pain. Do they embrace the unthinkable and end the pregnancy?

As a pastor I have counseled many would-be parents who have received bad news from in utero tests that suggest potential for physical or mental challenges, raising hard ethical questions. But a surprising number (in my statistically insignificant experience) proved to be false alarms. But how do we determine the worthiness of a life? How much intelligence or physical ability is enough? How little is not enough?

My cousin Sharon was born with Down syndrome, which made her fifty years of life very challenging. Yet in many ways she was the happiest, and certainly the most loving, among all of us Howells. Jean Vanier reported the following encounter in his L'Arche community, a community that cares for and lives with mentally challenged adults. He was in his office one day with a man who had come to visit—a very serious, rather glum man.

> There was a knock on the door. And before I could say "Come in," Jean Claude walked in. . . . Jean Claude technically would be Down syndrome. And Jean Claude shook my hand and laughed, and shook the hand of the other fellow and laughed, and went out laughing. And the man that had been in my office looked at me and said, "Isn't it sad, children like that?" . . . What was sad was that he was totally blind. He didn't see that Jean Claude was happy.[14]

I find myself writing a book about birth at a turning point in human history—and were I a betting man, I'd pick the side that suggests our technological prowess has hurried far ahead of the wisdom required to sort it all out. Siddhartha Mukherjee points out that "the most remarkable fact about human genomic engineering today is not how far out of reach it is, but how perilously, tantalizingly near."[15]

He worries, as we all should, that genetic manipulation "is like a headlong sprint into an abyss"—and he wonders if we realize the ways "our capacity to understand and manipulate human genomes alters our conception of what it means to be 'human.'"[16] He cites the ever-witty G. K. Chesterton, who oddly had the wisdom decades before the science emerged: "The students of heredity, especially, understand all of their subject except their subject."[17]

Will we really be able to create a master race or improve life on this planet? Or will we further denigrate the weaker members, the lowly and despised ones who very truly are, as Paul suggests, the indispensable ones (1 Cor. 12:23)? One year after Charles Darwin's death, Francis Galton published *Inquiries into Human Faculty and Development*, arguing for the selective breeding of the strongest, smartest, "fittest" humans, and he dubbed this quite *un*-natural selection "eugenics."[18] As late as 1980, Robert Graham, a millionaire, endowed a sperm bank (secured from accomplished people, like Nobel laureates) to sire people of high intellectual caliber. Thankfully, his business flopped.

Earlier in this book we dug into Andrew Solomon's work on children who were born dwarves, blind, or differently abled in various ways, or children who were the result of rape—and how parents cope and even celebrate children "who are not what they originally had in mind." His larger point is that "all offspring are startling to their parents; these most dramatic situations are merely variations on a common theme."[19] We must be similarly a bit surprising and disappointing to God, not being what God had in mind. But there is grace, mercy, and hope, isn't there?

The Christian norm, which should go without saying (and yet we need to say it to remind ourselves of what goes without saying), embodies the all-encompassing posture of welcome. Parents of deep faith and immense hospitality welcome children with all kinds of challenges. Their welcome is precisely the unconditional welcome we all crave, need, and need to extend. The child who isn't what the parents had in mind is just the test case, the shining example of whom God's good family embraces.

It is tempting for believers to yearn for and believe in the day when God will "redeem" such a child—when any child with any challenge will be healed and perfected. And yet this very impulse betrays our confusion about God's image in all of us and about how we define welcome. Ben Mattlin, a quadriplegic since birth, tells about attending the funeral service for a disabled friend—and why he left the service fuming. The pastor preached a trite sermon, and family members spoke of the way his deceased friend, confined so long to a wheelchair, is now free—walking and even playing basketball in the nude. Mattlin asked, quite simply, "Was he better off dead than disabled?" His personal confession was that his lifelong experience with disability has made him a more creative problem-solver; a die-hard optimist; and a more patient, tolerant, and flexible person. "My disability is part of who I am. Why couldn't my friend's family value the disabled man he'd become? How limited is this vision of life, and of the afterlife? Are there no wheelchairs in heaven? I'm not buying it. For me, if there is a heaven, it's not a place where I'll be able to walk. It's a place where it doesn't matter if you can't."[20]

ELEVEN

When Medicine Fails

Apart from infertility, there is a different kind of void, the crushing abyss that is the loss of a pregnancy, the death of what was or surely could have been a child: miscarriage, stillbirth, and other tragedies during childbirth or shortly thereafter. It could happen to any one of us—and it does happen every day, in every place.

They don't play music on the loudspeakers of the hospital when a child is lost. My mother-in-law endured four miscarriages and a stillbirth before her first child (now my wife) defied those odds and made it into the world. That was in the 1950s, when no one said anything, ever, about such an unspeakable loss—almost as if it were bad form or maternal failure. She carried those losses for decades, entirely isolated, in some hidden, dark place in her soul, and she finally spoke of those five losses with immense grief late in her life.

Fortunately, it is becoming more common to talk about these matters nowadays. A friend phoned me one day. She was at the hospital. They had just informed her she was miscarrying. Her husband was out of state on business. I arrived just as they had completed the "D&C," shorthand for dilation and curettage. We sat in silence until a friend of hers, in an unfittingly sunny mood, jauntily entered the room, hugged me and the would-be mom, and offered a cruelty I'm

134

sure she intended as comfort: "At least you weren't attached to it." An outburst of tears followed. "It" wasn't an "it" at all, and my friend was actually very much attached. The Bible tells us about Job's heartless friends Eliphaz, Bildad, and Zophar, as if to brace us: we will always have friends who are clueless about how to be friends during the moments we need friends the most.

A Well-Meant Alms of Breath

The Irish poet John O'Donohue, in his poem "For a Parent on the Death of a Child," helps us articulate the lonely sorrow that is the loss of a child. He explains how no one else can understand the feelings that your child "awoke in you," how you hold that child in your heart, how to become one and feel a love you've never felt before. Losing the child is being "inside a nightmare," and the child's absence may continue to be felt for a long time (the parent will feel this loss acutely, "will wear this like a secret locket"). O'Donohue encourages the parent to cry and then to ponder how their child is now an "unseen angel" who "parents [their] heart."[1] O'Donohue touches on hope, rightfully—although in the moment, if you're with someone (even yourself) who has suffered such loss, you stick with the grief, let it play itself out for however long. There's no stopwatch on grief. The recovery of hope will come in a few days, weeks, or months.

My fastidious, ridiculous self wants to correct O'Donohue on one little thing: departed children don't technically become angels, whom the Bible depict as messengers delivering daunting news. Yet isn't the fact of the lost child the most daunting news imaginable? Let a grieving mom have her solace that her lost child is an angel now. The wake of a loss is no time to theologize, especially if the theology is unintentionally sadistic or wrongheaded. Earnest Christians have a habit of offering a little gift of words we think will comfort anyone who's suffering. You know the trite, cruel messages: "She's in a better place." "God needed another angel." "It was God's will." These little sugary monstrosities misrepresent God and, if believed, run the risk of alienating the sufferer from God, just when that person needs God the most, by suggesting that God is a foe who ripped their beloved away from them.

Here is how James Russell Lowell responded (in poetry) to would-be comforters:

> Console if you will, I can bear it;
> 'Tis a well-meant alms of breath;
> But not all the preaching since Adam
> Has made Death other than Death.[2]

Lowell was trying to cope with the death of his daughter. Notice how the poem concludes:

> . . . Forgive me,
> But I, who am earthly and weak,
> Would give all my incomes from dreamland
> For a touch of her hand on my cheek.
> That little shoe in the corner,
> So worn and wrinkled and brown,
> With its emptiness confutes you,
> And argues your wisdom down.[3]

The little shoe lying on the floor, mute testimony to what was, and to what was lost, reminds me of the story Arthur C. Clarke told about Ernest Hemingway. At lunch with friends, Hemingway bet the table ten dollars each that he could craft an entire story in just six words. He collected his winnings after jotting this down on a napkin: "For sale: baby shoes, never worn."[4]

As a pastor, I find myself with people who have suffered terrible losses. All deaths are terrible, of course—but I'm thinking particularly of when it's the death of someone who's just too young. To prepare the survivors for the well-wishers coming by the house or to the funeral, I often hand them a photocopy of a napkin. Actually, it's a copy of a copy of a napkin. Years ago my mother was in a Cracker Barrel and noticed a really cute napkin. She picked it up, made copies, and sent them to my children, assuming they would delight in the cuteness as much as she did. Not the most insightful gift for adolescents—but well intended. I alert the grieving that people will hand them quite a few such napkins. Accept them for what they are—a woefully wobbly attempt to express some love, however awkward and misguided.

Miscarriage of Hope

The word *miscarriage* is a bit of a misnomer, as if a mistake (as in a "miscarriage of justice") has been made. Elise Erickson Barrett, in her thoughtful book *What Was Lost*, recalls dumb things people told her after she openly shared about her miscarriage: "God doesn't make mistakes." "God doesn't give you anything you can't handle." One well-meaning friend phoned her:

> She asked some questions, and upon discovering that I had completed only a year and a half of school and had a year and a half to go, she exclaimed, "Oh, Elise! . . . No wonder you had the miscarriage! God knew that having a baby and finishing school would have just about killed you! And his plans are always perfect." In the ache of my loss, everything about this correlation made me furious. . . . So God saw that my planner was full, and decided to kill my baby?[5]

The emotions that swirl around the unexpected cessation of pregnancy are like amusement park rides that jerk you in one direction and then another. After trying to become pregnant, you are! Such delight, rife with anticipation and some trepidation. The news is shared. Others are delighted too. Preparations begin. And then . . . Barrett reflects on the shock: "We are scared away from sex from adolescence on by the threat of a baby, we remember occasional alarmist articles in teen magazines about girls who got pregnant 'just from oral sex!'—no wonder it rarely occurs to us that it may, in fact, be possible to be pregnant without having a baby at the end of nine months. This is why, for many women, miscarriage comes as a terrible, unwelcome surprise, something they never knew they should fear."[6] A bizarre sense of alienation creeps in. A woman feels anger and mistrust toward her own body; this body she inhabits has betrayed her. Often, she blames herself. She wonders, "What did I do wrong?" The very question is a desperate grasp for a fragment of control when feeling very much out of control.

The ongoing bleeding punctuates, over and over, the horror and sorrow. Barrett tells us how a woman tries but fails to mash down all those old wives' tales, as if waking up in a cruel game of whack-a-mole in the soul: "Did I exercise too vigorously?" "Should I not have had sex?" "Did I eat the wrong stuff?" "Was it stress?" "Should I not have lifted that chair?"

Questions of identity and hope may rattle in her head. Our society values production—but she has failed to produce. In our culture, no matter how progressive we might think we are, we often value women more once they become mothers—but she isn't a mother now. Is there any hope? With a miscarriage, a vision of a future collapses, and the ability to dream of a future is shriveled as well.[7] And a woman dare not dwell on the hard facts: women who've miscarried face a 250 percent increased risk of depression and a 22 percent higher chance of divorce.[8]

Theological questions may also trouble some women: "Is God punishing me?" "Was I not good enough?" "Has God betrayed me?" "How can I pray to this God who abandoned me?" Yes, we know that God hears the silence that is our inability to pray as among our most profound prayers—but who can realize this in the dark? People say that time heals. The passing of time might just as easily make us bitter. One mom shared with me that her miscarriages helped her to become more ready for the child she eventually bore—not that God took the unborn ones or that the losses weren't keenly felt but that God used the time to refine her. Perhaps, yes? Maybe not? Hopefully?

Miscarriage isn't something that happens *to* you but *in* you. Many women will say, "My womb is a deathbed, my body a grave."[9] Serene Jones has reflected on the way many theologians think about love and death within God's own self, the Trinity, leading her to wonder if there is some consolation there for women who feel they have death within but have not died themselves. God the Father grieved the death of Christ his Son; death was in God. God was in some way responsible. Perhaps, then, we can sense that God experiences a kind of "solidarity with women grieving reproductive loss." Indeed, "God refuses to turn from us, even in the most brutal grip of tortured death and divine abandonment, and instead takes death into Godself." [10] The sorrow isn't erased, but feelings of isolation might be reduced if we know God is with us, that God has felt death within God's own self.

And so funeral liturgies are in order. Christians have been slow to get there. Other cultures, from ancient Hindus to pre-colonial New Guinea to modern Japan, have for a long time named and memorialized those lost to miscarriage. [11] I've had the holy privilege of officiating at several quiet liturgies of death and resurrection for families suffering miscarriage, stillbirth, and abortion.

Abortion is another kind of lost pregnancy, over which we should linger for just a moment. Many may want me to spill a lot of ink on this subject. Abortion has ended pregnancies, quite intentionally, for centuries and in every culture. In our day, abortion has—thankfully— been medicalized, and less happily, politicized. In the raging debates between pro-life and pro-choice citizens, and even people of faith, the real stories of real people get lost, and the palpable grief and sorrow go unnoticed. The women I have known who have had abortions are not ferocious banner-wavers with some steely resolve to slaughter innocents. There is often much grief, guilt, and even wondering about what might have been.

Pro-choice is a bit of a misnomer, as most feel they have no other choice and find themselves boxed into an impossible corner. Some women who are pro-choice struggle to grieve a miscarriage; does grief over a lost fetus imply the fetus matters enough to save? How do we as Christians frame the theological truths that life in the womb is somehow, in whatever complicated way, of God? And yet how can we be entirely attentive to and compassionate toward women whose dilemmas are fraught with sheer agony? Perhaps we can resonate with the words Brian Doyle wrote in his "Prayer for Women Who Endured Abortions": "Sisters, I stand before you without homily or lecture or opinion. I stand here with my hands extended in helpless prayer. I will never know your pain. I will never know your agony of spirit. I will never know the dark nights of your souls. I will never know the grinding fury of being lectured constantly by men who will never know what and how you felt." [12]

She Was Dead, but I Still Love Her

All sorts of pain and loss hover around the topic of birth. On March 30, 1853, Anna Carbentus gave birth to a son one year to the day after she had given birth to a stillborn child, whom she had named Vincent Willem van Gogh. This new child—a replacement?—was given the same name. Who can say how growing up in the same yard as a tombstone with your own name on it impacted this brilliant but deeply troubled person who never felt at home in the world?

My mother-in-law delivered a dead baby in 1957. A hushed cloud of denial prevented any kind of shared grief; that's just how things were back then. In her mid-eighties, coping with declining health, she jotted these words in her well-worn copy of Oswald Chambers's *My Utmost for His Highest*: "I have never been weaker or feebler than now, except when I carried a baby whom I learned had died in utero when I delivered her. She was dead, but I still love her. I named her Mary Grace recently, because I have never forgotten her."

Fortunately, stillbirths can now be spoken of, although people are unsure what exactly to say. I love the way Philip Turner began his sermon at the funeral for a stillborn child: "Brendan Joseph Albert Turner lived for seven months."[13] I have conducted quite a few funerals for families with such a child, named, and always to be remembered.

Some women will say that the joy of a baby can take away the pain of childbirth. If you don't believe it, ask a woman who had labored long and hard and then had no living child to hold, treasure, take home, and raise. Annie Proulx tells a story of a teenage girl who lived alone in a cabin in a remote part of Wyoming in 1885. Her young husband, Archie, had gone off on a cattle drive, assuming he'd return home in time for the birth of his first child. When the young woman woke one morning, it was cold and sleeting, and her back ached.

> By afternoon the backache was an encircling python and she could do nothing but pant and whimper, the steady rattle of rain dampening her moaning call for succor. She wriggled out of her heavy dress and put on her oldest nightgown. The pain increased to waves of cramping agony that left her gasping for breath, and on and on, the day fading

into night, the rain torn away by wind, the dark choking hours eternal. Another dawn came sticky with the return of heat and still her raw loins could not deliver the child. On the fourth afternoon, voiceless from calling for Archie, her mother, Tom Ackler, Tom Ackler's cat, from screaming imprecations at all of them, at god, any god, then at the river ducks and the weasel, to any entity that might hear, the python relaxed its grip and slid off the bloody bed, leaving her spiraling down in plum-colored mist. . . . She did not weep but, filled with an ancient rage, got away from the tiny corpse, knelt on the floor ignoring the hot blood seeping from her and rolled the infant up in the stiffening sheet. . . . She was driven to bury the child to end the horror of the event. She crept to the cupboard. . . . Her hand closed on the silver spoon, her mother's wedding present, and she thrust it into the placket neck of her nightgown. . . . She crawled out the door and toward the sandy soil near the river, where, still on hands and knees, still spouting blood, she dug a shallow hole with the silver spoon and laid the child in it, heaping it with sand and piling on whatever river stones were within reach.[14]

The average person would surely say that a miscarriage or a still-birth is nowhere near as awful as the death of a child who was born alive. But who can know such things? The Bible narrates, and grieves heavily, the deaths of infants. The first child Bathsheba bore after being taken by King David fell ill. David prayed constantly and fasted, refusing to rise from his prostrate position on the floor for seven days, until the baby died (2 Sam. 12:15–19). Pharaoh must have managed to drown quite a few Hebrew infants despite the chicanery of the midwives (Exod. 1:15–22).

Jesus's birth, celebrated with great joy through the centuries, was immediately accompanied by the horrific "slaughter of the innocents." Herod flew into a rage and killed all the little boys in the vicinity of Bethlehem (Matt. 2:16)—a haunting fulfillment of Jeremiah the prophet's vivid lament:

> A voice is heard in Ramah,
>   lamentation and bitter weeping.
> Rachel is weeping for her children;
>   she refuses to be comforted for her children,
>   because they are not. (Jer. 31:15, see also Matt. 2:18)

Cameraphoto Arte Venezia / Bridgeman Images

FIGURE 8. *Massacre of the Innocents* (1305–6), by Giotto di Bondone (1266–1337) / Scrovegni (Arena) Chapel, Padua, Italy

When Giotto painted the scene in the Scrovegni Chapel in Padua, Italy, he captured the sheer terror and agony that had to have been on the faces of the stricken mothers (see fig. 8).

We mentioned that when Jesus was born, God took on the great risk that is human life, the vulnerabilities of the human body that comes with no insulation, no guarantees, no fail-safe packaging. If you make it, if your child makes it, you always recall that you might not have made it, and you shudder as you ponder those who have loved and lost. Harriet Beecher Stowe watched helplessly as her toddler Charley died of cholera: "My beautiful, loving baby, so sweet, so full of life and hope . . . now lies shrouded, pale and cold. . . . I have just seen him in his death agony, looked on his imploring face when I could not help nor soothe nor do one thing, not one, to mitigate his cruel suffering, do nothing but pray in my anguish that he might die soon." And yet, not totally absorbed in her private grief, she turned in her heart to the plight of others: "Having experienced losing someone so close to me, I can sympathize with all the poor, powerless slaves at the unjust auctions."[15]

When My Heart's Dearest Died

Visit old cemeteries and make note of the dates and ages. So many children died young. Fairly often the mother died young too, often within a day or two of one of her children. Through most of history, and still in so many places, laboring mothers have been in grave peril. Jesus's name, *Yeshu'a*, means "Lord, help!"—a prayer every Jewish mother surely screamed to God during labor, pleading for the survival not just of the child but also of her own self. Rachel, the one with the lovely eyes for whom Jacob labored for fourteen years, died giving birth to her second son, Benjamin (Gen. 35:19). We might cut Jacob some slack if he was especially protective of her two boys.

Julius Caesar's wife, Cornelia, died giving birth to Julia, who also died while giving birth fifteen years later. Two of Henry VIII's six wives (Jane Seymour and Catherine Parr) died shortly after childbirth. Teddy Roosevelt's wife, Alice, died on Valentine's Day, 1884, two days after giving birth to their daughter. In his diary for that day, he drew a large cross and wrote, "She was beautiful in face and form, and lovelier still in spirit. . . . When my heart's dearest died, the light went from my life forever."[16]

Back then infection and blood loss, especially from panicked C-sections done without sterilization, made giving birth a high-risk, terrifying proposition. Death in childbirth still happens, even in major medical centers. Many will be surprised to learn that, in the United States, pregnancy-related deaths rose dramatically from 7.2 per 100,000 live births in 1987 to 26.4 in 2011, while during the same time period, the death rate in all other developed countries actually declined.[17] American women are three times more likely to die in childbirth than women in Canada and six times more likely than mothers in Finland. Four times as many black women in the United States die than white women. The reasons are manifold, complex, and not always clear—but the possibility of death in childbirth is very real.

And unspeakably sorrowful. An OB/GYN sat in my office and told me about delivering a baby—and then the mom developed toxemia, her liver ruptured, and she died. After many years, this tragedy still brought tears to his eyes.

Sown in Weakness

In the funeral liturgy of The Book of Common Prayer, we find the thought that "in the midst of life we are in death." In the mother's womb, the very place where God knits each of us together and makes life happen, and in the birthing room, a space (be it a fancy labor and delivery room or a one-room thatched house) that feels as sacred as any sanctuary, death happens. How do we think theologically about loss in what could have been birth?

We don't rush too swiftly to any cheerful good news. We linger over Good Friday and Holy Saturday patiently before we get to Easter Sunday. We listen to the pain; we feel the immense sorrow. But then, later on, at the nexus of a sufferer's emotional timing and God's merciful timing, we move toward hope. And the hope of the world, the hope for all who don't survive those months in the womb or those treacherous moments during and just after birth, resides in the infant who survived under unsanitary conditions, far from home, to the unlikeliest couple ever, attended to only by angels unseen. Jesus. His very name is that maternal cry, *Yeshu'a*, "Lord, help!" He is God incarnate, nicknamed Immanuel, meaning "God with us." He is the one who took on our flesh for a great many reasons, the heart of them all being to redeem our flesh.

Reflecting on that redemption, Paul spoke of how we sow a bare kernel of wheat: "What is sown is perishable, what is raised is imperishable. . . . It is sown in weakness, it is raised in power" (1 Cor. 15:42–43). God always takes what is small, what is unlikely, what has no power within itself, and miraculously brings forth life that is large and lush. The unformed ones, in God's good time, will be fully formed. The wounded ones will be fully healed. Maybe all we saw of a lost one was a grayish, fuzzy ultrasound. But what else did Paul tell us? "Now we see through a glass, darkly; but then face to face" (1 Cor. 13:12 KJV).

In my homily at my mother-in-law's funeral, I spoke of her stillborn child whom she never stopped loving—the one she named Mary Grace. If God's goodness is anywhere near as extravagant as the Bible assures us it will be, then Jean will have this little girl she never met fully restored to her. They will see each other, smile, embrace, and love. As Martin Luther puts it, "One must leave such situations to God and take comfort in the thought that he surely has heard our unspoken yearning and done all things better than we could have asked."[18]

I've preached the funerals of several infants. In preparing for one, a fellow pastor said to me, "He is more like God than he is like us now." Thankfully so, because this little boy, in his very short life, was poked, prodded, surgically cut, and radiated and medicated constantly. He endured more than a roomful of octogenarians have endured or could endure. I spoke of him as courageous.

At a few of these funerals, I have referred to Thérèse of Lisieux, who died in 1897, not as an infant but still far too young. Battling tuberculosis and other ailments, she always had an eerie longing for heaven and an understandable sense that her work was not yet accomplished. Shortly before dying, she wrote, "My mission is about to begin, my mission to make God loved as I love him, to give my little way to souls. If God grants my desires, . . . I will spend my heaven doing good upon earth."[19] If God's goodness is unlimited, and if God calls each of us to some holy missional work, isn't there a way to envision an infant's mission to make God loved as continuing beyond the harrowing loss we feel here—and that this love for God is the only real healing for any of us?

Finally, let's return to the sermon Philip Turner preached at the service for the stillborn child who had lived seven months in utero. When the boy was delivered, they realized he had spina bifida, a cleft palate, and clubfeet. "From the beginning he was terribly wounded. . . . He died as he lived, quiet and unseen, cuddled in his mother's womb. When he was born, his parents held him, wept, called him by name, and said goodbye; but from now on they will know him only by his absence." Then Turner spoke of at least a partial fulfillment of this little boy's ministry to all of us: "We can see ourselves in him. We can see that one day we will be as helpless and wounded as he was from the day of his conception. We can see that our lives, like his, are short, and that their transfiguration is as dependent upon the grace and power of God as is his. . . . The fathomless love of God is all that Brendan has. We delude ourselves if we believe we have more."[20]

This is Turner's ending, not overly triumphant but lovely and imaginatively hopeful: "It is Brendan and millions like him who will lead us all into the kingdom of heaven. That great company which no one can number will be led by the little ones. . . . There is a great company of children dancing and singing, and Jesus walks behind them like a good shepherd. Because they are so protected, they can skip freely and without care before the throne of God."[21]

PART 4

OUR NEW BIRTH

TWELVE

Adoption

For many people, maybe more than we realize, there is a plot twist in their birth stories. A separation occurs shortly after delivery, a complication forever lodged in the psyche of the mother and the child: adoption. A mother endures months of physical stirrings, discomfort, and pain—and is back home shortly thereafter, a mom but not a mom. There will be no nursery, no waking up in the middle of the night, no cradling. A child enters the world and is placed in a different home with parents who weren't involved in conception, pregnancy, or delivery.

Does the child experience this as a rejection? Think of how many movie and novel plots, and maybe the thoughts of people you've known, revolve around an adopted child determined to find the elusive birth parents. Kelly Nikondeha, in her thoughtful and theologically profound book about adoption, reflects on her own quest, as an adult, to seek out the parent who gave her up for adoption: "We want that dark corner illuminated. We imagine our own transformation at the revelation of our true origin. What goodness might be unlocked, what possibility unleashed?"[1]

Adoption inevitably carries with it feelings of immense ambiguity. Is it a happy outcome? Or is there sorrow? A peculiar wound opens up for the children who live forever with the nagging reminder that they were given up, abandoned maybe, and yet with the gratitude that someone else chose to engage in the ultimate hospitality of taking, keeping, raising, and loving them.

This reminds us of how things have always been between human beings and God. Jesus was "given up," not by Mary but years later by his closest friends—and he even felt abandoned by God his Father. He endured what he endured, though, to bring us into God's family as adopted sons and daughters. "When the fullness of time had come, God sent his Son, born of a woman, . . . so that we might receive adoption as children" (Gal. 4:4–5 NRSV). This is the marvelous way Scripture speaks about adoption: God takes what may be regarded as the less-than-ideal way to be born and to grow up, and God says, "This is the ultimate expression of my love for you and your belonging to me and to one another."

The Foundling in Literature

There is considerable cultural intrigue around the notion of having a biological parent you don't know and being raised by someone else. Adopted children appear in the plots of many books, plays, and movies. How many people through history were adopted? Leonardo da Vinci, Babe Ruth, Edgar Allan Poe, John Lennon, Eleanor Roosevelt, James Baldwin, Steve Jobs, Leo Tolstoy, Lafayette, the Roman emperors Trajan and Hadrian, Aristotle, Confucius, and Nelson Mandela. Queen Esther of the Bible was adopted. Superman was adopted, and so was Buddy, who was an elf at the North Pole but then finally located his father, Walter, in New York. The profoundly moving film *Lion* tells the story of Saroo, adopted by an Australian family, finally managing to locate his mother in rural India. The themes of vulnerability, love, and reconciliation in such stories fascinate all of us, including those who've never adopted or been adopted.

Consider Harry Potter: Albus Dumbledore delivered him as a baby to the Dursleys after the murder of young Harry's parents. Of course, Harry wasn't the only thing that Dumbledore left behind him on this occasion: he also protected Harry with strong magic to keep him safe from Lord Voldemort and his Death Eaters while Harry lived with the Dursleys—until he came of age on his seventeenth birthday.

In Sophocles's *Oedipus Rex*, thanks to Oedipus's relentless curiosity, he learns the truth about being adopted. Henry Fielding's *The History of Tom Jones* is the story of a "foundling," a baby smuggled into the bed of the benevolent squire Thomas Allworthy. And we can't forget Eppie, the young girl who proved to be the redemption of George Eliot's surly miser, Silas Marner. More recently, M. L. Stedman's *The Light between Oceans* and Celeste Ng's *Little Fires Everywhere* have picked up on the trope of an abandoned child. The persistence of this foundling theme—which has never once happened in the vicinity of anyone in my fairly large circle of acquaintances—intrigues, apparently tapping into the nexus of fear and hope, vulnerability and resilience in all of us.

Adoptions in literature and the arts are sometimes more institutional: we may love the musicals *Oliver!* and *Little Orphan Annie*. And what story of an orphan is more compelling than John Irving's stellar *Cider House Rules*, where Dr. Larch not only cares for orphans but reads to them from great literature before bedtime, bidding them off to sleep with these immortal, encouraging words: "Goodnight, you princes of Maine, you kings of New England."[2]

The Biblical Mandate

The Bible offers us a variety of scenarios when it comes to defining family. Adopted children are at the heart of God's plans of salvation! Jochebed had no choice but to relinquish little Moses, depositing him in a basket and pushing it out into the Nile to float downstream to . . . she had no idea where, and she clung desperately to hope against hope. Her relinquishment delighted the Pharaoh's daughter—and then, years later, led to the liberation of Israel from Egypt. Abraham, desperate for the heir God had promised, adopted Eliezer of Damascus and then fathered Ishmael, the son of Sarah's Egyptian maid, Hagar—with harrowing, painful results.

Both Old and New Testaments are adamant about the inescapable moral mandate to take care of orphans. Moses commands the Israelites to assume full care for orphans in their midst (Deut. 24:17), and James, the brother of our Lord, declared that religion that is "pure and faultless is this: to look after orphans and widows in their distress" (James 1:27 NIV). Historically, the church has often, but not always, risen to the challenge. When Jesus soothingly promised, just before he strode out into the darkness of Gethsemane, "I will not leave you orphaned" (John 14:18 NRSV), he was thinking not only of his relationship with his followers but also of what they would do for others who were or felt orphaned.

Old-style orphanages, perhaps thankfully, no longer exist in America. Still, around the world, orphanages continue, and while sometimes they feed into foster programs in more developed countries, they also feed into permanent poverty in poorer regions.

I have seen this firsthand, as my family has been involved for years with an orphanage in Nakuru, Kenya; we've sponsored a child each year, and our daughter has visited and volunteered there several times. More recently we've become involved with ZOE,[3] a creative and powerfully effective ministry to orphans in Kenya. Instead of just housing or feeding them, the program provides training in work skills and basic start-up provisions so they can grow small businesses and provide for younger siblings; it's all about empowerment. This isn't charity and doesn't leave them to their own devices either. This organization walks alongside them and encourages them. Rather than fostering dependency or independence, it fosters interdependency. The results are inspiring when an orphan becomes part of a family of orphans heading their own families in entrepreneurial, life-giving, dignity-building ways.

A Different Kind of Belonging

Nikondeha offers a picturesque retrospective on what being adopted was about: "A woman scooped me out of the white-wicker bassinet in the viewing room of the adoption agency and claimed me as her own. Her physical emptiness prepared the way for my fullness."[4] Then, pondering the woman who bore her, she tries to fathom if her giving her child up was a rejection? Or rather a relinquishment?

Some might rush to condemn a mother who "abandons" her baby. Some might politicize adoption, pointing to Mother Teresa, who spoke against abortion and pleaded with young women who were pregnant, "Give us the child." But isn't there always a wrinkle in the story—that a woman who did not have to carry the child for so long actually did, and at considerable physical cost? What if surrendering your child at birth is a loving relinquishment—not a rejection but a humble acquiescence in the face of crushing circumstances? Why did mothers at the famed eighteenth-century Foundling Hospital in London leave not only their babies but also tokens of love, like jewelry or a poem?

With adoption we get a glimpse of a different kind of belonging. Nikondeha suggests that adoption is "like a sacrament, that visible sign of an inner grace. It's a thin place where we see that we are different and yet not entirely foreign to one another. We are relatives not by blood, but by mystery."[5] In God's church we are always united not by blood but by the water of baptism. Our inclusivity, at least the inclusivity toward which we aspire, can make physical kinship, nationality, and ethnicity look far too narrow. God's way is always wider, more encompassing, and downright sacramental.

How wonderful is it then that when Scripture tries to explain to us what it is to belong to God's Body, the church, our inspired authors landed on adoption as their powerful image? "To all who received him, who believed in his name, he gave power to become children of God; who were born, not of blood nor of the will of the flesh nor of the will of man, but of God" (John 1:12–13). In Romans 8, Paul probes this notion of yearning for and receiving adoption; this un-earned, graciously received status enables us to pray—and intimately. "You have received the spirit of sonship. When we cry, 'Abba, Father!' it is the Spirit himself bearing witness with our spirit that we are children of God" (Rom. 8:15–16)—and in God's ultimate future it gets even better, as we adopted ones become heirs, "fellow heirs with Christ" (v. 17), who is our brother, again by adoption.

The disciples knew of God as "Father to the fatherless" (Ps. 68:5). So they must have blushed and been confused and deeply moved when Jesus, during his final meal with them, said "I will not leave you orphaned" (John 14:18 NRSV); the Greek, *orphanous*, is sometimes translated "desolate." We might wonder if people among John's first readers were disowned by their biological parents because of their countercultural belief in Jesus. Throughout history, how many children were virtually orphaned by parents who didn't appreciate the way of Jesus? Saint Francis of Assisi's father, Pietro Bernardone, sued his son, disowned him, and then for the rest of his days refused to speak to him and even spat in his direction if he passed him on the street. God is the true Father of all who are fatherless.

The fatherless need God the Father. I saw a Kenyan preacher move some young orphans to tears by explicating the Lord's Prayer and the love we find in realizing that God is indeed our "Father," even if we have lost our earthly fathers. Those of us with fathers and those of us who are fathers were simultaneously engaged and enveloped in that same family love.

The Costs of Adoption

Latecomers into the family aren't always warmly welcomed. Paul opened up Christ's family to people who had not been to synagogue, who had eaten the wrong foods, and who had never been circumcised. People with centuries-old family connections to the patriarchs of old, people who had clung in holy obedience to God's laws suddenly witnessed a huge influx of siblings into their family, newcomers who were not disobedient to the law so much as just plain ignorant of it. And then these newcomers were exempted from it![6]

But the God of the Scriptures is always about radical hospitality. And what greater act of hospitality can there be than welcoming someone very different, and entirely unrelated by blood, into one's home and for good? Such parents are most certainly not "reproducing." They aren't even producing. They are simply welcoming, sacrificing, loving. Kevin Wright, a pastor and close friend of mine who was adopted, puts it like this: "I believe in a God who has adopted us all into his family. In a world in which flesh and blood means so much to us—so much so that we spend millions of dollars each year on fertility treatments and medicine to improve our chances of conceiving—we are reminded that to produce a son or daughter is costly. Indeed, it cost God the price of his son."

THIRTEEN

Remember Your Baptism

Moments after you are born, after the first cry, after the cord is cut, and after a little celebrating, you get your first bath. You aren't really dirty, coated as you are in that precious holy womb stuff. Countless baths will follow. The most important of the tens of thousands of baths to follow, the bath of all baths, is your baptism. Some won't get this bath until they are grown—or ever. But for many Christians, baptism happens not too long after birth. It's sort of a completion of the birth that seals you as born of more than just your parents; it's your first rite of passage, your official entry into the universal and eternal Body of Christ.

Even if a child is born to parents who aren't baptismally inclined, after birth you have to do something. The first words a Muslim infant hears, whispered into one ear seconds after birth, are "There is no God but Allah, and Muhammad is his messenger," and then a little honey and a bit of date are rubbed onto the palate so the child's first taste of life is sweet. In *The Lion King* the newborn Simba was anointed with coconut juice and then raised high in the arms of Rafiki at the pinnacle of Pride Rock, to the acclamation of all the creatures of the jungle (while everyone sings "The Circle of Life").

Water upon More Water

Jesus, like all Jewish boys, was circumcised on his eighth day. This ceremony, called the bris, is a sacred moment of ritual, tradition, prayer, and celebration. Family and friends gather for the official naming of the child. The mohel, a professionally trained expert in circumcising, welcomes the boy with the words *baruch ha-ba*, "blessed is the one who has arrived." Blessings follow, with wine, and then the foreskin is severed. Baby girls, bumping up against the first of many glass ceilings to come, do get a festive meal and joyful welcome, although never quite as big a deal as the bris.

The application of water to an infant, minutes after birth or at their baptism days or weeks later, may be a bit superfluous. The newborn's body is already more than 80 percent water! And the largely amphibious child has just emerged from a watery voyage, just now unsubmerged from an entirely watery place where it lived quite contentedly immersed for months. Water is simply who we are. God's blessing comes to you through what you already are. Grace overflowing, fitting, natural.

In the sacrament of baptism we use water, which reminds of us the water we drink or a beautiful lake or how we wash. If you are drawn to the sea, if you while away time by a river, if a stream makes any painting or photograph more lovely to you, if a rain shower somehow calms your soul, it likely is because water is your home, your origin, the sacramental blessing of God in baptism.

If you are a spiritually focused person, you might think of every bath you take as a recollection of your baptism, a remembering of who you are and where you came from. That historic admonition, "Remember your baptism, and be thankful," even if you can't summon up the memory in your mind's eye, does make space for this grand act of grace to be grace for you. Martin Luther, without pondering the percentage of water that we all are, and yet having bathed and baptized his own children, regularly said, "There is no greater comfort on earth than baptism." When he was in despair, he would remind himself, "I am baptized, and through my baptism God, who cannot lie, has bound himself in a covenant with me."[1]

On several occasions, I've received frantic phone calls from parents of a newborn under considerable duress, asking if I can hustle

to the neonatal unit and baptize their baby. This rush to baptize is
far less common than it once was. Through much of history, a child
who died without receiving the sacrament of baptism was thought
to be barred from heaven—a tragedy worse than the tragic enough
loss of life. Medieval midwives were even given permission to fulfill
the priestly duty of baptism, and many did so even when the child
had not even fully emerged from the womb.

We can rest assured that if an unbaptized infant dies, God is not
so petty as to hurl the little one into eternal perdition. We can also
rest assured that, no matter how evolved and correct our thinking
about all this might be, children today (just like children long ago)
are born into a very small world in which religious commitments,
and thus religious anxieties, swirl. Parents may think they will let
a child choose for him- or herself about faith. But the very air the
child breathes from day one is infused with beliefs, doubts, worries,
apathy, perhaps some theological wisdom and calm, and probably a
fair amount of hackneyed and obtuse spiritual confusion.

While even the holiest families face daunting challenges as a baptized child grows up in a culture with indifferent, hostile, or confused
perspectives on Christianity, it is appalling to observe the trivializa-
tion and perversion of baptism. In modern American culture, infant
baptisms have taken on a kind of sentimental aura, even a giggly
cuteness. One new dad bumped into me at a ball game and said, "We
need to get the baby done." Søren Kierkegaard, with hilarious and
blistering sarcasm, narrated a typical baptism in nineteenth-century
Denmark:

> It is a young man, we can imagine him with more than ordinary abil-
> ity, knowledge, interested in public events, a politician, even taking
> an active part as such. As for religion, his religion is . . . that he has
> none at all. To think of God never occurs to him, any more than it
> does to go to church. . . . He almost fears that to read God's Word at
> home would make him ridiculous. This same young man who feels
> no need of religion . . . marries, then he has a child. And then what
> happens? Well, our young man is, as they say, in hot water about this
> child; in the capacity of presumptive father he is compelled to have
> a religion. And it turns out that he has the Evangelical Lutheran reli-
> gion. So they notify the priest, a young lady holds the infant's bonnet

coquettishly, several young men who also have no religion render the
father the service of having, as godfathers, the Evangelical Christian
religion, while a silken priest with a graceful gesture sprinkles water
three times on the dear little baby and dries his hands gracefully with
the towel—and this they dare to present to God under the name of
Christian baptism.[2]

And far worse, who could forget that horrific scene at the end of *The
Godfather* where, even as holy vows are made and the water applied
to the godchild in the church, the Corleone family's enemies are being
brutally murdered just a few blocks away.

What Good Is Baptism?

What is the point of this rite, this sacrament of baptism when applied
to an infant? Saint Augustine understood our sacraments as "visible
words."[3] What God says to us when we baptize an infant is: You are
part of the Body of Christ; you are gifted with the Holy Spirit; you
are joined in union with Christ; forgiveness is real. Geoffrey Wainwright writes that the "theological coloration" of infant baptism is
that it is "a striking sign of the prevenient grace of God, who acted
first for [humanity's] redemption in Jesus Christ and who is at work
from the start to bring individuals to salvation."[4] God's visible word
in the water is, "I knew you before you knew God or really anybody
or anything, even when you lived in your mom's watery womb."
This grace is unmerited, unchosen, unavoidable. And this gracious
bestowal isn't just past or present but also future. Jürgen Moltmann
suggests that "Christian baptism is eschatology put into practice,"
and so it is "hope in action."[5] God says, "You have a future with me."

In my Methodist tradition, we don't do private baptisms. In baptism, you're entering a community. And the community pledges to
support you. Rowan Williams pictures it this way: "Baptism brings
you into the neighbourhood of other Christians."[6] You'll need them.
And they'll need you. P. T. Forsyth explores the usefulness of baptism: "We ask, What good does Baptism do for me or that child?
instead of, What is the active witness and service the Church renders
to the active Word of Christ's Gospel in the baptism of young or old?

Sacraments are necessary for the health of the Church. Baptism is necessary for the weal of the Church." Forsyth adds that this same baptism is "necessary for the world the Church has to convert."[7] Or as Karl Barth puts it, "In each baptism, the Church crosses its own frontiers into the territory of the people which walks in darkness."[8] As trivialized as baptisms may seem, they have the potential to help those who do not know or love the Lord Jesus to get a clear glimpse of what God's grace is all about.

I have baptized more than two thousand infants. Sometimes I'm just moving along, being sure I do the liturgy properly and don't flub up. But many times I pause and look closely into the face of the child I've been handed by nervous, eager parents. So much beauty, so much need, so vulnerable, so beloved. In the face of each infant, I see a tangible reflection of what God became for us in Christ. When God thought, "I want them to know me," God didn't come as a warrior or a giant or a queen. God came as an infant—tiny; vulnerable; entirely needy; and requiring much tenderness, love, and care. If only the world could see and understand. If only the church could remember and trust.

I am sympathetic to theologians, some of them my very favorites, who prefer infants not be baptized, who believe that the Bible and rational thinking press us to wait until the child believes, until he or she is striving to be obedient to God. Barth and Moltmann in particular perceived quite rightly that if we baptize infants, we inevitably wind up with a nationalistic, culturally entangled church that is clueless in the face of evil.[9] They knew: they barely survived the atrocities of baptized Nazis slaughtering the Jews and trampling on the holiness of God's church. Even if we baptize infants, Barth's main point holds: "Believing is something which no one else . . . can do for us: not even the most believing parents, the strongest Christian [sibling], the most vital community, the whole Church, the full chorus of believers in every century and country."[10]

Because baptized individuals and then whole societies of baptized people can find themselves co-opted, unwittingly or quite cheerfully, by the forces of evil, it is wise for the church to include in the rites of baptism a section of renunciations or even "exorcisms" that renounce Satan and the world. The moral mandate attached to every

newborn is that life is sacred, and therefore we shout a firm no to any
politics or movements that denigrate life or harm anybody anywhere.
Alexander Schmemann spoke of these baptismal renunciations with
words that pinpoint what we must do constantly: "The exorcisms
mean this: to face evil, to acknowledge its reality, to know its power,
and to proclaim the power of God to destroy it. . . . The first act
of the Christian life is a renunciation, a challenge. No one can be
Christ's until [he or she] has, first, faced evil, and then become ready
to fight it. How far is this spirit from the way in which we often 'sell'
Christianity today!"[11]

Of course, verbal renunciations and invocations of divine power
won't crush the forces of evil. But their wiles are at least exposed,
and the church family is awakened once more to our constant task,
which the baptized infant will hopefully grow up to participate in:
waging holy combat against all that is not of God.

Upon This Rock

Just as the triumph is ultimately in God's hands, and our privilege is
to share in the labor and ride in on God's coattails, so it is when the
priest blesses the water in baptism. The prayer does not change the
water into some magic elixir. God's presence sanctifies the water—
both the water in the font and the water that makes up the majority
of the body of the one being baptized. God descends, no matter the
virtue or lack thereof in the priest's private life or in the quality of
his or her liturgical performance.

And yet, or because of this, we are careful about baptizing. We
don't pour the water from a milk jug or a paint bucket. And we don't
pour the water into a dog food bowl or a sippy cup. Many church
sanctuaries feature permanent, solid, well-crafted vessels to hold the
water. We might call it a font—a misnomer really, since the water rests
quite still in the bowl. Protestants typically put the font up front, at
the center of our attention. Even if we've not witnessed a baptism
in many months, we are reminded of our own baptisms. Catholics
place the font at the entrance of the church, as if you can't get into
the place without being reminded that this is the way into the church

Chris Light, CC BY-SA 4.0 / Wikimedia Commons

FIGURE 9. Baptismal font in San Rufino (Assisi)

and life with God. You're invited to dab a little of the baptismal water onto your head, a lovely practice and mute sermonette to the water that you are and the water that saves.

Wherever I travel, I check out the font in each church I enter. I have my favorites. Years ago, I visited the Georgenkirche in Eisenach,

Germany, where Johann Sebastian Bach was baptized on a wintry day in 1685. Four of his older siblings had already died of various causes. Alex Ross tried to imagine the scene: "I pictured Bach's parents looking on at the baptism, and wondering whether he would live. They had no idea."[12] Indeed, as Ross thought this, he was listening to one of Bach's cantatas, recorded in that very church, three centuries after the baptism.

Then there's the cathedral San Rufino in Assisi. The font just inside and to the right must hold a world's record: not one, not two, but three official saints were baptized there (see fig. 9): Saint Francis, of course, his friend Saint Clare, and also Saint Gabriele dell'Addolorata. On top of that, an emperor, Frederick II, was baptized in this overachieving font.

And finally, not far from my home: the basilica at Belmont Abbey features a rough-hewn stone font that is the ultimate in repurposing. In antebellum North Carolina, this rock served as the trading block on which slaves were auctioned. Decades later, the stone was adapted to serve as the church's font. Its inscription reads: "Upon this rock, men were once sold into slavery. Now upon this rock, through the waters of baptism, men become free children of God."

FOURTEEN

You Must Be Born Again

Jesus, who underwent the most stupendous transition in all of history (God being born), tells us that we must be born again. What could he have meant? Why is it that preachers, who've talked for centuries about being born again, virtually ignore birth itself when theologizing about being born again? And can all we've explored in this book about birth, life in utero, labor, and baptism help us understand being born again—and then actually discover ourselves to be born again?

The famous evangelist George Whitefield, who preached eighteen thousand times between 1736 and 1770 and who talked tens of thousands of people into getting born again, was once asked, "Why do you go on and on about being born again?" He replied, "I do so because you must be born again." He spoke from experience. As an adolescent, he recalled, "I was brutish from my mother's womb. Lying, filthy talking, and foolish jesting I was much addicted to."[1]

Yet all along he felt regular movings of the Spirit, provoking him to tears of remorse. At Oxford, with the brothers Wesley, he committed to the highest ideals of a holy life. But even a strictly religious lifestyle didn't satisfy; his heart was "barren and dry."[2] "God showed me that I must be born again, or be damned! I learned that a [person] may go to church, say prayers, receive the sacrament, and yet not be a Christian. . . . True Christianity is a union of the soul with God, and Christ formed within us—a ray of divine light was instantaneously

163

darted into my soul, and from that moment, and not till then, did I know I must become a new creature."[3]

Feeling waves of emotion, groaning through the night, and finally casting himself entirely on God's mercy, Whitefield felt the redemption, liberation, and joy of the new birth he would preach about for the rest of his life. The intense, emotional freight of what he understood as being born again was widely experienced. He reported that as he preached people fell to the ground, "dropp'ed down, as tho' shot with a Gun." He and others couldn't explain it, but those who had been born again knew that the feeling was "a spiritual, as well as a corporeal feeling."[4]

In modern times, Billy Graham traveled to every corner of the globe preaching this "new birth," which for him was "saving knowledge of Jesus Christ," which means accepting Christ as your Savior and commencing a personal relationship with God. The emotional wave was experienced at the close of every revival meeting when the crowd would sing "Just as I Am" (also the title of Graham's autobiography), and instead of people dropping down "as tho' shot with a Gun," they would come on down to the altar for prayer.

Graham, a pastor to presidents, once asked Lyndon Johnson, "Mr. President, have you ever personally, definitely received Jesus Christ as your Savior?" After gazing across the landscape of his ranch, Johnson said, "Well, Billy, I think I have. . . . I guess I've done it several times." Graham wasn't sure about this: "It's a once-for-all transaction. You receive Christ and he saves you. His Spirit bears witness with your spirit that you're a child of God."[5] People Graham preached to in stadiums, and those watching via television, were always invited to bow their heads, right on the spot, and pray the simple prayer of faith. In that moment of acceptance, "You become a child of God, adopted into His family forever. He also comes to live within you and will begin to change you from within. No one who truly gives his or her life to Christ will ever be the same."[6]

John Wesley preached constantly on the new birth and its "marks": faith, hope, and love. His worry was over the tepid to vapid responses to baptism in people's lives. Yes, they'd been sprinkled, but nothing changed. So, nestled near the intersection of his doctrines of justification and sanctification was his understanding of the new birth, regeneration: "Justification implies only a relative, the new birth a real change. God in justifying us does something *for* us; in begetting us again, He does the work *in* us."[7] Edgar Young Mullins, a nineteenth-century Baptist preacher, clarified: "It is a change wrought by the Holy Spirit. It is accomplished through the instrumentality of the truth. It is a radical change of the moral and spiritual disposition. It is a change in which the soul is recreated in the image of Christ."[8]

What fascinates here is that people who talk about being born again rarely, if ever, link it to birth itself. Whitefield, Wesley, and Graham were probably out preaching on the road somewhere and never witnessed children being born. We might ponder for a moment, in the light of all we've explored in this book, what "born again" might mean for us if Jesus had the keen wisdom to invite us to reflect on the quirky and lovely realities of our first, physical birth.

How is discipleship like birth? Let's look once more to the words of the writer Anne Enright. Though she has no evident interest in religion, after had a child she noted, "My past life has become foreign to me. . . . I am prey, for the rest of my life, to every small thing."[9] Isn't this what being with Jesus, a child who came out of his mother, is like? The past is laughably past. Every small thing, devoted to this Jesus, matters.

The Conversation with Nicodemus

Let's look at the most famous of all Bible passages that speak of being born again: John, chapter 3, the conversation about an unexpected new birth—carried on between two men, via the pen of another man. They may not have thought about what we might find hidden in their words—but we suspect and hope that C. S. Lewis was right to suggest that "an author doesn't necessarily understand the meaning of his own story better than anyone else."[10] Can't the Spirit speak through Scripture so that we find fresh perspectives—in our case based on the knowledge of women who've delivered children, midwives who've delivered them, or what we now know that the author of John, or Jesus himself, would not have known?

Nicodemus, a prominent member of the highest governing body in Judaism, approaches Jesus at night (John 3:1–14). Does the darkness symbolize ignorance, untruth, or evil? Is it for stealth? But wasn't the womb dark? Isn't it curious that, in explaining this new birth to Nicodemus, Jesus speaks of being born of water and the Spirit. We might dart to John the Baptist's statement that he baptizes with water, but Jesus will baptize with the Spirit (John 3:11). But recall your first birth. You were in water. Then you emerged, gasping for air, for a breath—or we can say "spirit," as the Hebrew *ruah* and the Greek *pneuma* both mean air, and then by extension, spirit. It's always water, and then the spirit when getting born.

That you "must" be reborn intrigues. The Greek, *dei*, implies throughout John's Gospel something of a divine necessity, a holy compulsion. Jesus "had" (*dei*) to pass through Samaria—not because it was the shortest route but because he was on a saving mission to the Samaritan woman. You must be born again. It's not *must* as in "You must do your homework" or "You must report for jury duty." It's more like "You must come to my birthday party!" or "You must come with me to the hospital to see Fred before he dies." It's love; it's a deeply personal, can't-miss-it necessity. And yet, you just might miss it. Jesus is no autocrat. You must be born again, but you might not be—although Jesus, tenderly offering, luring, and leading, is literally dying for you to be born again.

Commentators expend their energy on the Greek *anōthen*, which can mean "again" or "from above." Many think Jesus meant "from above"—that is, from God—but Nicodemus heard it as "again." Hence his confusion. But Jesus didn't correct him—and they weren't chatting in Greek in the first place! They would have been conversing in Aramaic, which doesn't have this double meaning. It's lovely that John theologizes about it and prompts us to parse out that our new birth is of divine origin. One of Jesus's signature proclamations was not that we should become more mature and well-aged but that we should become like children (Matt. 18:3). How do we imagine getting smaller and younger?

I baptized a man who was dying of pancreatic cancer. As the water dripped off his forehead and down his cheeks, he looked at me and said, "I feel lighter. I feel younger." Could there be some holy, crazy miracle of the sort imagined in David Wilcox's funny song in which he envisions living life in the other direction? Die first, get it out of the way. Then you can enjoy your retirement, while you're still young. But then you get bored, you want to be useful, so it's time to go to work—and the first day you get a gold watch! Yet after a while, money's not so important to you. It's time to go to college, then high school. Eventually, you find yourself learning simpler and simpler things, and you realize that anything worth saying slips past language, so you quit talking. You're taking yourself a lot lighter. You *are* a lot lighter—until you decide to go out "as a glimmer in someone's eye."[11]

Let's follow Jesus's invitation to regress to younger days, much younger days, even prenatal days. Jesus tells Nicodemus that unless you are born *anōthen* you cannot see the kingdom. Not: you cannot get into heaven. But: you cannot see the kingdom. In the womb before you were born the first time, you had fully formed eyes, but you could not see. This life with Jesus is always eye-opening, a new kind of seeing. John Wesley expresses this well: "Before a child is born into the world he has eyes, but sees not; he has ears, but does not hear. . . . It is then only when a man is born that we may say he begins to live. . . . While a man is in a mere natural state . . . he has, in a spiritual sense, eyes and sees not. . . . He has ears, but hears not. . . . But as soon as he is born of God, there is a total change."[12]

The new birth Jesus offers us is not so much an emotional experience but a realization, a clarity of vision. I begin to see with God's eyes. I see the world, others, and myself as God sees. What does my body look like? Am I too fat, too scarred, not pretty enough? Or is this body truly a temple of the Holy Spirit (1 Cor. 6:19)? Is the other guy too muscular, too dumb, too scary? Or is he too another portable sanctuary? Is the world my playground, or a terrifying place to be avoided, or God's good creation, awaiting redemption as eagerly as I am? Didn't God tell the prophet that God sees not as we see (1 Sam. 16:7)?

This clarity also leads to a new way of reading Scripture. Martin Luther narrates his dramatic personal turning to faith and mercy: "I meditated day and night on 'The righteous shall live by faith.' I began to understand that justice in which man lives by the gift of

God, by faith, is understood passively as that whereby the merciful God justifies us by faith. . . . I felt myself born anew, the whole face of the Scriptures was altered."[13] Nicodemus was a Scripture scholar. Jesus invited him, and invites us, to pick up the spectacles of new birth and see God's Word in fresh, newly born ways.

A Miraculous Event

The heart of Jesus's surprising notion of being born again is this: you can't grit your teeth and be born the first time, and you can't do so for being born *anōthen* either. In October 1955 I didn't think, "Hmm, nice day to be born; let's do it." Rather, my birth was an event I didn't choose. Even mothers have zero ability to turn their microscopic zygotes into breathing, squalling people. Birth happens to us, and being born again happens in us. Rudolf Bultmann, reflecting on Jesus's reply to Nicodemus's search for salvation, clarifies that "the condition can only be satisfied by a miracle. . . . It suggests to Nicodemus, and indeed to anyone who is prepared to entertain the possibility of the occurrence of a miraculous event, that such a miracle can come to pass."[14]

God knows we could all use a miracle. John Calvin, probing Jesus's thoughts on being born anew, believes that "he means not the amendment of a part but the renewal of the whole nature. Hence it follows that there is nothing in us that is not defective."[15] It's not our defectiveness so much as our brokenness. A sense of failure bedevils us. I've been betrayed by others or more likely by myself. Sara Bareilles put these words on the lips of Jenna in the musical *Waitress*: "Most days I don't recognize me. . . . I'm not anything like I used to be. . . . She is gone but she used to be mine."[16] Jenna is pregnant, regrets how she got there, but finally forges into a new life.

Elie Wiesel wryly suggests that when God made Adam, "God gave him a secret—and that secret was not how to begin but how to begin again."[17] This God-given mystery is required for a new birth: we are as incapable of new birth as a camel is of squeezing through the eye of a needle, as Sarah was of bearing Isaac in her old age, as Mary was of conceiving before having known Joseph, or even as Jesus was of climbing out of the tomb on Easter morning. He didn't escape. God raised him.

Given the ways preachers like Whitefield and Graham conducted revivals seeking new births that were marked by a swoon of emotion, it's important to realize that Jesus didn't ask Nicodemus to feel anything. There are, of course, intense feelings at birth. The mother giving birth may be overwhelmed with an intensity of joy or with a broad spectrum of emotions. The feelings mother and child share in childbirth are the pains, the excruciating squeezes, the tearing of flesh, and sometimes the breaking of bones. Could Jesus have imagined such agony when pressing us toward a new birth? Jesus courageously embraced pain and invited us to follow. Paul, imprisoned and beaten multiple times within an inch of his life for following Jesus, writes, "When we cry, 'Abba! Father!' it is the Spirit himself bearing witness with our spirit that we are children of God . . . provided we suffer with him" (Rom. 8:15–17). No wonder we prefer a happy, emotional rebirth at a revival over the costly discipleship that is the new life Jesus has in mind for us. It isn't the feeling but the fact of the new birth and the hard facts of union with Jesus in a world puzzled or hostile to his ways.

We are feeling people; so what might the new birth feel like—apart from the cost and pain? Ben Witherington can guide us:

> If we wish to push the birth analogy a bit, we might say that one's labor before the birth may be long and painful or short and relatively uneventful. It may be attended by many or witnessed by none other than oneself. The new birth may involve a dramatic turning from darkness to light, or a quiet assurance after long searching that one truly is a child of God. The time of crossing the river may be noted on the occasion, or only realized long after one is on the other shore. One may know when one's spiritual birthday is, or, on the other hand, the records and remembrance of it may be lost.[18]

By now, of course, we see that Jesus wasn't asking Nicodemus to behave a little better. It's radical, a total shift of focus, priorities, behaviors, and habits. Bultmann explains it perfectly: "Rebirth means . . . something more than an improvement in man; it means that man receives a new *origin*, and this is manifestly something which he cannot give himself."[19] My first birth defined my origin as a Howell. I have the DNA; I favor my dad; I am who I am. How could I come by a new and different origin? Let's look to Saint Francis of Assisi (see fig. 10).

> After fitting in and even excelling as a child and youth, enviably popular, chic and cool, Francis heard the call of Jesus. Taking the Bible quite literally, picking up whatever Jesus said or did and putting it on his to-do list for the day, Francis divested himself of his advantages, including his exquisite, fashionable clothing, which he gave away to the poor. His father, Pietro, a churchgoing, upstanding citizen, took exception, locked his son up for a time, and then sued him in the city square. Giotto's fresco in the basilica where Francis is buried shows a stark naked Francis, handing the only thing he has left, the clothes off his back, to his father. But his eyes are fixed upward, where we see a hand appearing to bless him from up in the clouds. At this moment, Francis declared, "Until now I have called Pietro di Bernardone my father. But, because I have proposed to serve God, I return to him the money on account of which he was so upset, and also all the clothing which is his, wanting to say from now on: 'Our Father who are in heaven' and not 'My father, Pietro di Bernardone.'"[20]

This is a biblical moment, if we have regard for passages that suggest "You have been born anew, not of perishable seed but of imperishable, through the living and abiding word of God" (1 Pet. 1:23) or that Jesus has "come to set a man against his father, and a daughter against her mother" (Matt. 10:35).

Another vivid, biblical moment: Jonathan Wilson-Hartgrove narrates his daddy's departure from the Ku Klux Klan. He'd been raised to participate in the Klan, which was the deepest abiding passion of all the men in his family. When he exited the Klan, Jonathan's mother took his clan robes, cut up the white fabric, and made dress shirts out of them. His granddaddy, uncles, and cousins never spoke to anyone in his family again. The price of shedding an evil perversion of Christianity? "To hold on to their view of the world and of themselves, they had to disown their flesh and blood."[21]

New birth is a real change, a transition as dramatic as the most dramatic transition ever: being born. R. C. Sproul, a renowned evan-

Public Domain

FIGURE 10. *Renunciation of Worldly Goods*, 1297–99, by Giotto di Bondone (1266–1337)

gelical, offers a sustained theological perspective on this sort of experience. For him, the phrase "born again Christian" is redundant, as there is no other kind; to be a Christian you must be born again.[22] No one is born a Christian; the reborn Christian exhibits a palpable change in disposition and passions: he or she "cares for the things of God and desires to seek God. Now there is an affection for God that was not there before. It is far from perfect, but it is real."[23]

The great revivalists could point to more than emotion and disposition as the fruit of their campaigns. Stuart Henry describes what unfolded after Whitefield was done preaching: instead of being "nominally Christian," people were transformed "from beasts into saints, and from a devilish [nature], to be made partakers of a divine nature."[24] The communities where John Wesley and Jonathan Edwards preached witnessed a measurable drop in drinking and unemployment. Husbands were better husbands. Children learned to read. The poor were cared for. Even illness diminished.[25]

Y'all Together Must Be Born Again

Individuals are born again. But it's a mistake to psychologize this rebirth or whittle it down to a merely individual, private shift. As Jesus describes being born again, it doesn't quite match up to what we think about salvation—as in getting to go to heaven. Being born again means being caught up into the reign of God, finding ourselves in the thick of what God is doing with and through God's people, the church. When Jesus tells Nicodemus "You must be born again," the "you" is plural (John 3:7 NIV)—so Jesus isn't speaking just to this one man but to his people and even to us. And when we are born the first time, we are but one in a zillion or one of a couple dozen in a hospital nursery. We are not alone; we are in this with others, always.

Our best commentators help us understand John 3. D. A. Carson writes, "For a man like Nicodemus, entering the kingdom of God did not have to do with the transformation of an individual character but with participation in the resurrection life of the new order God would powerfully bring about at the end of history."[26] Marianne Meye Thompson writes something even more grounded in what happens in birth the first time: "Even as one is born into a family, tribe or people, so being 'born again' entails identifying with a new people complete with its own characteristic practices and commitments."[27]

New birth is not a solo feeling but entails practices and commitments; it entails others. Our new cues come from Scripture, worship, and every means of grace. "Like newborn babes, long for the pure spiritual milk, that by it you may grow up to salvation" (1 Pet. 2:2). The first practice is baptism, the water and spirit sacrament. Rightly we baptize infants, reminding us of the day these wee ones were even smaller and younger. In the early church, the newly baptized, as they emerged from the water, were wrapped in a new robe and given a little taste of milk and honey. And our second practice, the Eucharist, dares to suggest that just a little food and drink, the amount a baby might eat, is just enough.

We engage in the full package of radically different Christian dispositions and activities. We love enemies. We deliver aid instead of sending it, as Wesley wisely advised. We do not lay treasure up on earth (Matt. 6:19); we expect nothing less than the conversion of the pocketbook. When we have a dinner party, we invite not those who can invite us in return but "the poor, the maimed, the lame, [and] the blind" (Luke 14:13). Worship is a must. Daily prayer is our sustenance. Sacrificial giving becomes a great delight. Perhaps we loosen our grip on private ownership and hold what we have in common, to ensure no one is in need (Acts 2:44; 4:32). After all, you have a new origin; you are no longer your own.

With others we join in the subversion that is the labor of the family of God on earth. We disturb our cities (Acts 16:20). We turn the world upside down and act contrary to the decrees of the emperor (17:6). We live in communities not afraid to love and welcome the stranger, the shunned, or the despised. We dare to go out into the world with love in order to make a few dents in a world desperate for Jesus's new birth but hardened against it—or determined to stay in what feels like the warmth and security of a womb that isn't the liberated, glorious life God is eager for all to enjoy.

Perhaps being born again is like the discovery so many new moms make, articulated beautifully in John O'Donohue's words we pondered earlier: "Once it began, you were no longer your own. / A new, more courageous you offered itself."[28]

Epilogue

Usually at this point, the author will thank those who helped in the writing and improvement of the book. I'll get to that in a minute. For the moment, it occurs to me that pondering all that we've explored here elicits immense gratitude. Given that I began as the twinkle of someone's eye and lived an aquatic, microscopic life for weeks, and that I could easily not have survived and no one would have known or grieved, I am grateful that I exist. I was in my mother, a petite woman with whom I always had a strained relationship. She died shortly after I finished writing this book, and we had never reconciled very well. And yet, she delivered me. Must have been harrowing. How does this knowledge induce a fresh gratitude for her?

Dumbfounded by this, I am awed in fresh ways by the gospel. God somehow became incarnate through Mary, who survived the agony of birth, for no other reason than to love and be loved and plant hope deeply in me and in all of us. My gratitude and love for such a God have grown considerably as I am just in awe. I try to be tender with God, and with all who've been born. I'm more in awe of myself, as I was so much like God when I was born. I'm more hopeful too, as I once was so very close to God—so I might be again.

I am grateful for my children, who seem so much tinier and yet so much larger as I contemplate where they once were and where they are now. I see them now as evangelists who've brought me closer to God and even to those who can't or haven't had children. I see our implacable, shared bonds as once-birthed people living forward with unpredictable plots, twists, and turns. Hopefully we are eager to follow and enjoy the one, the Christ, who was born not to protect us or fix everything but just to be with us.

And so I suppose I also remember my baptism and am so thankful. The realization of all the miracle and mercy, the chance and steady presence of God awakens in me a curious sense that I genuinely have been born again. Knit together, called, and graced. I hope you too are, with me, so very grateful.

Notes

Introduction

1. Mark Sloan, *Birth Day: A Pediatrician Explores the Science, the History, and the Wonder of Childbirth* (New York: Ballantine, 2009), 32.

2. Wenda R. Trevathan, *Human Birth: An Evolutionary Perspective* (New Brunswick, NJ: Transaction, 2011), 171.

3. Adam Rutherford, *A Brief History of Everyone Who Ever Lived: The Human Story Retold through Our Genes* (New York: The Experiment, 2017), 1.

4. Henry David Thoreau, *"Walden" and "Civil Disobedience"* (New York: Vintage Books, 2014), 25.

5. P. D. James, *The Children of Men* (New York: Warner, 1992), 7.

6. Carl Sandburg, *Remembrance Rock* (New York: Harcourt Brace Jovanovich, 1948), 7.

7. William Wordsworth, "Michael," in *The Norton Anthology of Poetry* (New York: Norton, 1975), 593.

8. Celeste Ng, *Little Fires Everywhere* (New York: Penguin, 2017), 122.

9. Walter Isaacson, *Leonardo da Vinci* (New York: Simon & Schuster, 2017), 422.

Chapter 1 In My Mother's Womb

1. Hans Urs von Balthasar, *Explorations in Theology III: Creator Spirit*, trans. Brian McNeil (San Francisco: Ignatius, 1993), 17.

2. *Forrest Gump*, directed by Robert Zemeckis (Hollywood: Paramount Pictures, 1994), DVD.

3. Adam Rutherford, *A Brief History of Everyone Who Ever Lived: The Human Story Retold through Our Genes* (New York: The Experiment, 2017), 4.

4. Rutherford, *Brief History of Everyone Who Ever Lived*, 34.

5. Mark Sloan, *Birth Day: A Pediatrician Explores the Science, the History, and the Wonder of Childbirth* (New York: Ballantine, 2009), 37.

6. *The World according to Garp*, directed by George Roy Hill (Burbank, CA: Warner Bros., 1982), DVD.

7. Joseph Hart, "Come Ye Sinners, Poor and Needy," 1759, https://hymnary.org/text/come_ye_sinners_poor_and_needy_weak_and.

8. Frederick Buechner, *Wishful Thinking: A Theological ABC* (New York: HarperOne, 1993), 95.

9. Sloan, *Birth Day*, 170–71.

10. Walter Isaacson, *Leonardo da Vinci* (New York: Simon & Schuster, 2017), 72, 261.

11. Mary Oliver, "I Happened to Be Standing," in *A Thousand Mornings: Poems* (New York: Penguin, 2012), 3.

12. Art Garfunkel, "All I Know," side B, track 1 on *Angel Clare*, Columbia, 1973.

13. Henri Nouwen, *Our Greatest Gift: A Meditation on Dying and Caring* (New York: HarperCollins, 1995), 18–19.

Chapter 2 My Birthday

1. John O'Donohue, "For Your Birthday," in *To Bless the Space between Us: A Book of Blessings* (New York: Doubleday, 2008), 52.

2. William Manchester, *The Last Lion: Winston Spencer Churchill*, vol. 1, *Visions of Glory, 1874–1932* (New York: Dell, 1983), 36.

3. Manchester, *Last Lion*, 1:108.

4. C. S. Lewis, "Membership," in *The Weight of Glory and Other Addresses* (New York: Collier, 1980), 110.

5. Volker Ullrich, *Hitler: Ascent, 1889–1939*, trans. Jefferson Chase (New York: Knopf, 2016), 15.

6. Wenda R. Trevathan, *Human Birth: An Evolutionary Perspective* (New Brunswick, NJ: Transaction, 2011), 120.

7. Mark Sloan, *Birth Day: A Pediatrician Explores the Science, the History, and the Wonder of Childbirth* (New York: Ballantine, 2009), 250.

8. Carl Sandburg, *Remembrance Rock* (New York: Harcourt Brace Jovanovich, 1948), 8.

9. Sloan, *Birth Day*, 25.

10. Dorothy Day, *The Long Loneliness* (New York: Harper & Row, 1952), 139.

11. Leo Tolstoy, *Anna Karenina*, trans. Joel Carmichael (New York: Bantam, 1960), 758.

12. David F. Ford, *Self and Salvation: Being Transformed* (New York: Cambridge University Press, 1999), 18.

13. Walter Isaacson, *Leonardo da Vinci* (New York: Simon & Schuster, 2017), 72, 261.

14. Julian of Norwich, *Showings*, trans. Edmund Colledge and James Walsh (Mahwah, NJ: Paulist Press, 1978), 295, 299.

15. Arthur C. Brooks, "Do You Like Your Name?," *New York Times*, May 31, 2018.

16. Austen Ivereigh, *The Great Reformer: Francis and the Making of a Radical Pope* (New York: Picador, 2014), 83.

17. John Allen, "On Pope Francis's First Year," Radio Boston, March 25, 2014; cited in Ivereigh, *Great Reformer*, 83.

18. Leonardo Boff, *Francis of Rome and Francis of Assisi: A New Springtime for the Church*, trans. Dinah Livingstone (Maryknoll, NY: Orbis, 2014), 1.

19. Ivereigh, *Great Reformer*, 84.

20. Annie Dillard, *Holy the Firm* (New York: Harper & Row, 1977), 25.

Chapter 3 Unchosenness and Being Chosen

1. Malcolm Gladwell, *Outliers: The Story of Success* (New York: Little, Brown, 2008), 15–34.

2. Carl Sandburg, *Remembrance Rock* (New York: Harcourt Brace Jovanovich, 1948), 6–7.

3. Siddhartha Mukherjee, *The Gene: An Intimate History* (New York: Scribner, 2016), 367.

4. Trevor Noah, *Born a Crime: Stories from a South African Childhood* (New York: Random House, 2016), 26.

5. Amos Oz, *A Tale of Love and Darkness* (Orlando: Harcourt, 2003), 190.

6. Bill Bryson, *Shakespeare: The World as Stage* (New York: HarperCollins, 2007), 32.

7. Siddhartha Mukherjee, *The Emperor of All Maladies: A Biography of Cancer* (New York: Scribner, 2011), 292–93.

8. Mukherjee, *Gene*, 387.

9. Martin Heidegger, *Being and Time*, trans. J. Macquarrie and E. S. Robinson (London: SCM, 1962), 174–76; Heidegger, *Existence and Being* (South Bend, IN: Gateway, 1949), 34–52.

10. Jon Levenson points out that the verb *hasaq* implies an affair of the heart, a burning passion; God in effect "falls in love" with Israel. Levenson, *The Love of God: Divine Gift, Human Gratitude, and Mutual Faithfulness in Judaism* (Princeton: Princeton University Press, 2016), 40.

11. Paul Tillich, "You Are Accepted," in *The Shaking of the Foundations* (New York: Scribner's Sons, 1948), 154–63.

12. Walter Brueggemann, *Chosen? Reading the Bible amid the Israeli-Palestinian Conflict* (Louisville: Westminster John Knox, 2015), 26.

13. Richard Dawkins, *The Selfish Gene* (New York: Oxford University Press, 1989), v.

14. Dawkins, *Selfish Gene*, 3.

15. Jonathan Sacks, *The Dignity of Difference* (London: Continuum, 2002), 53.

16. Barry Estabrook, *Tomatoland: How Modern Industrial Agriculture Destroyed Our Most Alluring Fruit* (Kansas City, MO: Andrews McMeel, 2012), 35.

17. Robert Plomin, *Blueprint: How DNA Makes Us Who We Are* (New York: Penguin, 2018), 147.

Chapter 4 Mary, Mother of Our Lord

1. Rowan Williams, *A Ray of Darkness* (Cambridge, MA: Cowley, 1995), 15.

2. Richard Rohr, *The Good News according to Luke* (New York: Crossroad, 1997), 85.

3. Sebastian Brock, *The Luminous Eye: The Spiritual World Vision of Saint Ephrem* (Kalamazoo, MI: Cistercian, 1985), 25.

4. Williams, *Ray of Darkness*, 13.

5. Martin Luther, "The Magnificat," trans. A. T. W. Steinhaeuser, in *Luther's Works* (St. Louis: Concordia, 1956), 21:328.

6. Thomas F. Torrance, *Incarnation: The Person and Life of Christ* (Downers Grove, IL: IVP Academic, 2008), 43.

7. Alan Jacobs, *The Narnian: The Life and Imagination of C. S. Lewis* (New York: HarperCollins, 2005), xxi–xxiv; Charles Taylor, *A Secular Age* (Cambridge, MA: Belknap, 2007), 35; James Kugel, *The Great Shift: Encountering God in Biblical Times* (New York: Houghton Mifflin Harcourt, 2017), 51.

8. Brock, *Luminous Eye*, 33.

9. Roland H. Bainton, ed., *Martin Luther's Christmas Book* (Minneapolis: Augsburg, 1948), 12.

10. Quoted from a conversation with Robert McAfee Brown in *Spirituality and Liberation: Overcoming the Great Fallacy* (Philadelphia: Westminster, 1988), 136.

11. Herbert O'Driscoll, *Portrait of a Woman* (New York: Seabury, 1981), 23.

12. William Wordsworth, "The Virgin," in *The Collected Poems of William Wordsworth* (Hertfordshire, UK: Wordsworth Editions Limited, 1994), 518.

13. Rohr, *Good News according to Luke*, 70.

14. Bainton, *Martin Luther's Christmas Book*, 20.

15. Maggie Ross, *The Fountain and the Furnace* (New York: Paulist Press, 1986), 80.

16. Matthew Fox, *Passion for Creation: The Earth-Honoring Spirituality of Meister Eckhart* (Rochester, VT: Inner Traditions, 2000), 336.

17. Bainton, *Martin Luther's Christmas Book*, 21.

18. Rohr, *Good News according to Luke*, 72.

19. Jeremy Troxler, "Mentoring the Mother of God," in *Mentoring for Ministry: The Grace of Growing Pastors*, ed. Craig T. Kocher, Jason Byassee, and James C. Howell (Eugene, OR: Cascade, 2017), 8.

20. In Augustine's "Nativity Sermon," quoted by Thomas Aquinas, *Summa Theologica* III, Q35, A6.

21. Rachel Marie Stone, *Birthing Hope: Giving Fear to the Light* (Downers Grove, IL: IVP Books, 2018), 127.

22. Carlo Carretto, *Blessed Are You Who Believed*, trans. Barbara Wall (Tunbridge Wells, UK: Burns & Oates, 1982), 75.

Chapter 5 The Birth of Jesus

1. Madeleine L'Engle, *A Cry Like a Bell* (Wheaton: Shaw, 2000), 55.

2. Roland H. Bainton, ed., *Martin Luther's Christmas Book* (Minneapolis: Augsburg, 1948), 33.

3. Cited and discussed extensively by Thomas F. Torrance in *Incarnation: The Person and Life of Christ* (Downers Grove, IL: IVP Academic, 2008), 58–75.

4. Torrance, *Incarnation*, 77.

5. Annie Dillard, *Holy the Firm* (New York: Harper & Row, 1977), 47.

6. "Lo, How a Rose E'er Blooming," trans. Theodore Baker, *The United Methodist Hymnal* #216, https://hymnary.org/text/lo_how_a_rose_eer_blooming.

7. Samuel Wells, *A Nazareth Manifesto: Being with God* (West Sussex, UK: Wiley & Sons, 2015), 12.

8. Wells, *Nazareth Manifesto*, 241–43.

9. Jean Vanier, *From Brokenness to Community* (New York: Paulist Press, 1992), 16.

10. Wells, *Nazareth Manifesto*, 29–30, 84.

11. Mike Slaughter, *Christmas Is Not Your Birthday: Experience the Joy of Living and Giving Like Jesus* (Nashville: Abingdon, 2011), xi.

12. Sarah Howell-Miller, "The Atheist Christmas Carol (Christmas Is for Everyone)," December 24, 2017, https://sarahshowell.wordpress.com/2017/12/24/the-atheist-christmas-carol-christmas-is-for-everyone.

13. J. Richard Middleton, *A New Heaven and a New Earth: Reclaiming Biblical Eschatology* (Grand Rapids: Baker Academic, 2014), 24.

14. Madeleine L'Engle, "First Coming," in *The Ordering of Love: The New and Collected Poems of Madeleine L'Engle* (Colorado Springs: WaterBrook, 2005), 242.

15. Chiara Frugoni, *Francis of Assisi: A Life* (New York: Continuum, 1999), 115.

16. Rowan Williams, *A Ray of Darkness* (Cambridge, MA: Cowley, 1995), 3.

Chapter 6 Jesus's First Days

1. George Eliot, *Silas Marner* (New York: Bantam, 1981), 112.

2. These words are from the extended book version: J. R. R. Tolkien, *Sauron Defeated*, ed. Christopher Tolkien (Boston: Houghton Mifflin, 1992), 38.

3. Elie Wiesel, *Night*, trans. Marion Wiesel (New York: Hill & Wang, 2006), 65.

4. Raymond E. Brown, *The Birth of the Messiah* (Garden City, NY: Doubleday, 1977), 203–4.

Chapter 7 Why Have Children?

1. John O'Donohue, "For a Mother-to-Be," in *To Bless the Space between Us: A Book of Blessings* (New York: Doubleday, 2008), 56.

2. Madeleine L'Engle, *And It Was Good: Reflections on Beginnings* (Wheaton: Shaw, 1983), 18.

3. O'Donohue, "For a Mother-to-Be," 56.

4. Brian Doyle, *How the Light Gets In: And Other Headlong Epiphanies* (Maryknoll, NY: Orbis, 2015), 19.

5. Elizabeth Norton, *The Hidden Lives of Tudor Women: A Social History* (New York: Pegasus, 2017), 10.

6. Elaine Scarry, *On Beauty and Being Just* (Princeton: Princeton University Press, 1999), 3.

7. Susan L. Crockin and Howard W. Jones, *Legal Conceptions: The Evolving Law and Policy of Assisted Reproductive Technologies* (Baltimore: Johns Hopkins University Press, 2010), 275.

8. Meaghan O'Connell, *And Now We Have Everything: On Motherhood before I Was Ready* (New York: Little, Brown, 2018), 22.

9. April Dembosky, "Nurse Calls Cops after Woman Seeks Help for Postpartum Depression. Right Call?," Shots: Health News from NPR, February 7, 2018, https://www.npr.org/sections/health-shots/2018/02/07/582394435/nurse-calls-cops-after-woman-seeks-help-for-postpartum-depression-right-call.

10. Andrew Solomon, *Far from the Tree: Parents, Children, and the Search for Identity* (New York: Scribner, 2012), 1.

11. Solomon, *Far from the Tree*, 5.

12. Emily Perl Kingsley, "Welcome to Holland," in *Chicken Soup for the Mother's Soul: 101 Stories to Rekindle the Spirits of Mothers*, ed. Jack Canfield, Mark Victor

Hansen, Jennifer Read Hawthorne, and Marci Shimoff (Deerfield Beach, FL: Health Communications, 1997), 113–16.

13. Kingsley, "Welcome to Holland," in *Chicken Soup for the Mother's Soul*, 116.

14. Martin E. Marty, *The Mystery of the Child* (Grand Rapids: Eerdmans, 2007), 1.

15. Marty, *Mystery of the Child*, 24.

16. Søren Kierkegaard, *Fear and Trembling and the Sickness unto Death*, trans. Walter Lowrie (Princeton: Princeton University Press, 1954), 38.

17. Jim Forest, *Love Is the Measure: A Biography of Dorothy Day* (Maryknoll, NY: Orbis, 1994), 47.

18. Stanley Hauerwas, *A Community of Character: Toward a Constructive Christian Social Ethic* (Notre Dame, IN: University of Notre Dame Press, 1981), 165.

19. Roland Bainton, *Here I Stand: A Life of Martin Luther* (New York: Mentor, 1950), 226.

20. Jürgen Moltmann, *The Church in the Power of the Spirit*, trans. Margaret Kohl (Minneapolis: Fortress, 1993), 229.

21. Homer, *Iliad*, I.423, trans. Stanley Lombardo (Indianapolis: Hackett, 1997), 13.

22. Rachel Hollis, "Bikini Picture," The Chic Site, March 31, 2015, https://the chicsite.com/2015/03/31/bikini-picture.

23. Graham Greene, *The End of the Affair* (New York: Penguin, 1962), 110.

Chapter 8 Having Children

1. Anne Lamott, *Bird by Bird: Some Instructions on Writing and Life* (New York: Anchor, 1994), 87.

2. Angela Garbes, *Like a Mother: A Feminist Journey through the Science and Culture of Pregnancy* (New York: Harper Wave, 2018), 101.

3. Anne Enright, *Making Babies: Stumbling into Motherhood* (New York: Norton, 2004), 56.

4. Siddhartha Mukherjee, *The Gene: An Intimate History* (New York: Scribner, 2016), 181.

5. Karl Barth, *Church Dogmatics*, III/4, trans. A. T. Mackay, T. H. L. Parker, Harold Knight, Henry A. Kennedy, John Marks (Edinburgh, UK: T&T Clark, 1961), 278.

6. Meaghan O'Connell, *And Now We Have Everything: On Motherhood before I Was Ready* (New York: Little, Brown, 2018), 53.

7. Garbes, *Like a Mother*, 77.

8. Enright, *Making Babies*, 28.

9. Jennifer Worth, *Call the Midwife: A Memoir of Birth, Joy, and Hard Times* (New York: Penguin, 2002), 9.

10. Madeleine L'Engle, "The Risk of Birth, Christmas, 1973," in *The Weather of the Heart* (Colorado Springs: Crosswicks, 2001), 39.

11. Courtney Martin, "The Liminal Space before Giving Birth," On Being, July 22, 2016, https://onbeing.org/blog/the-liminal-space-before-giving-birth.

12. Tina Cassidy, *Birth: The Surprising History of How We Are Born* (New York: Grove Press, 2006), 161.

13. Rachel Marie Stone, *Birthing Hope: Giving Fear to the Light* (Downers Grove, IL: IVP Books, 2018), 51.

14. Leo Tolstoy, *Anna Karenina*, trans. Joel Carmichael (New York: Bantam, 1960), 753–54.

15. Mark Sloan, *Birth Day: A Pediatrician Explores the Science, the History, and the Wonder of Childbirth* (New York: Ballantine, 2009), 94.

16. The notion that suffering is noble has been cruelly misused by slave owners and many others through history. Suffering in itself may have a nobility, but it may be an injustice crying out for rectification.

17. Lionel Shriver, *We Need to Talk about Kevin* (New York: Harper Perennial, 2003), 75.

18. Brigitte Jordan, *Birth in Four Cultures: A Crosscultural Investigation of Childbirth in Yucatan, Holland, Sweden, and the United States*, 4th ed. (Long Grove, IL: Waveland, 1993), 33.

19. Margaret F. Myles, *A Textbook for Midwives* (Baltimore: Williams & Wilkins, 1971), 698.

20. Jordan, *Birth in Four Cultures*, 22–41.

21. Jordan, *Birth in Four Cultures*, 22–41.

22. Lauren F. Winner, *Wearing God: Clothing, Laughter, Fire, and Other Overlooked Ways of Meeting God* (New York: HarperOne, 2015), 149.

23. "Announcement of a Baby Son for the Duke and Duchess of Cambridge," The Royal Household, April 23, 2018, https://www.royal.uk/announcement-baby -son-duke-and-duchess-cambridge?page=10.

24. Mary Costello, *Academy Street* (New York: Farrar, Straus & Giroux, 2014), 82.

25. Wenda R. Trevathan, *Human Birth: An Evolutionary Perspective* (New Brunswick, NJ: Transaction, 2011), 107.

26. O'Connell, *And Now We Have Everything*, 111.

Chapter 9 The First Days after Birth

1. Samuel Wells, *Incarnational Ministry: Being with the Church* (Grand Rapids: Eerdmans, 2017), 107.

2. Julian of Norwich, *Showings*, trans. Edmund Colledge and James Walsh (Mahwah, NJ: Paulist Press, 1978), 295, 297.

3. John Goldingay, *The First Testament: A New Translation* (Downers Grove, IL: IVP Academic, 2018), 693.

4. Daniel A. Hughes, *Attachment-Focused Parenting: Effective Strategies to Care for Children* (New York: Norton, 2009), 12.

5. Meaghan O'Connell, *And Now We Have Everything: On Motherhood before I Was Ready* (New York: Little, Brown, 2018), 138.

6. Mark Kurlansky, *Milk! A 10,000-Year Food Fracas* (New York: Bloomsbury, 2018), 5.

7. Anne Enright, *Making Babies: Stumbling into Motherhood* (New York: Norton, 2004), 48, 49, 53.

8. Angela Garbes, *Like a Mother: A Feminist Journey through the Science and Culture of Pregnancy* (New York: Harper Wave, 2018), 145.

9. Wenda R. Trevathan, *Human Birth: An Evolutionary Perspective* (New Brunswick, NJ: Transaction, 2011), 181.

10. Bernard of Clairvaux, *On the Song of Songs I*, trans. Kilian Walsh (Kalamazoo, MI: Cistercian, 1979), 53–68.

11. Trevathan, *Human Birth*, 136.

12. Dietrich Bonhoeffer, *Psalms: The Prayer Book of the Bible* (Minneapolis: Augsburg, 1974), 9.

13. Maryanne Wolf, *Proust and the Squid: The Story and Science of the Reading Brain* (New York: Harper Perennial, 2007), 82.

14. David Eagleman, *The Brain: The Story of You* (New York: Vintage, 2015), 7–9.

15. Annie Dillard, *An American Childhood* (New York: Harper & Row, 1987), 11.

16. Kimberly Harrington, *Amateur Hour: Motherhood in Essays and Swear Words* (New York: Harper Perennial, 2018), 21.

17. Dar Williams, "The One Who Knows," track 7 on *Many Great Companions*, Razor & Tie, 2010, used by permission.

18. Sally Bedell Smith, *Elizabeth the Queen: The Life of a Modern Monarch* (New York: Random House, 2012), 4.

19. Paul Mariani, *Gerard Manley Hopkins: A Life* (New York: Penguin, 2008), 425.

20. Raymond Carver, "Late Fragment," in *All of Us: The Collected Poems* (New York: Knopf, 1998), 294.

21. Jennifer Worth, *Call the Midwife: A Memoir of Birth, Joy, and Hard Times* (New York: Penguin 2002), 267.

22. Brian Doyle, *How the Light Gets In: And Other Headlong Epiphanies* (Maryknoll, NY: Orbis, 2015), 19.

23. Eagleman, *The Brain*, 11.

24. Donna Jackson Nakazawa, *Childhood Disrupted: How Your Biography Becomes Your Biology, and How You Can Heal* (New York: Atria, 2015), 25.

Chapter 10 Infertility and Medicine

1. Elizabeth Hagan, *Birthed: Finding Grace through Infertility* (St. Louis: Chalice, 2016), 22.

2. Hagan, *Birthed*, 74.

3. Hagan, *Birthed*, 158.

4. Rowan Williams, *Being Christian: Baptism, Bible, Eucharist, Prayer* (Grand Rapids: Eerdmans, 2014), 25, 27.

5. Gilbert Meilaender, *Bioethics: A Primer for Christians* (Grand Rapids: Eerdmans, 1996), 42.

6. Allen Verhey, *Reading the Bible in the Strange World of Medicine* (Grand Rapids: Eerdmans, 2003), 300.

7. James Joel Shuman, *The Body of Compassion: Ethics, Medicine, and the Church* (Boulder, CO: Westview, 2000), 7.

8. Drew Pearson, *Aberdeen Daily News*, November 9, 1953.

9. Meilaender, *Bioethics*, 23.

10. Jennifer Weiss, "Now It's Melissa's Time," *New Jersey Monthly*, May 26, 2007.

11. Christine Hauser, "4,000 Eggs and Embryos Are Lost in Tank Failure, Ohio Fertility Clinic Says," *New York Times*, March 28, 2018, https://www.nytimes.com/2018/03/28/us/frozen-embryos-eggs.html.

12. Susan L. Crockin and Howard W. Jones, *Legal Conceptions: The Evolving Law and Policy of Assisted Reproductive Technologies* (Baltimore: Johns Hopkins University Press, 2010), 388.

13. Crockin and Jones, *Legal Conceptions*, 63.

14. Jean Vanier, "The Wisdom of Tenderness," *On Being*, with Krista Tippett, May 28, 2015, https://onbeing.org/programs/jean-vanier-the-wisdom-of-tenderness.

15. Siddhartha Mukherjee, *The Gene: An Intimate History* (New York: Scribner, 2016), 467.

16. Mukherjee, *The Gene*, 11–12.

17. G. K. Chesterton, *Eugenics and Other Evils* (London: Cassell, 1922), 66, cited in Mukherjee, *The Gene*, 17.

18. Mukherjee, *The Gene*, 64.

19. Andrew Solomon, *Far from the Tree: Parents, Children, and the Search for Identity* (New York: Scribner, 2012), 5.

20. Ben Mattlin "Valuing Life, Whether Disabled or Not," NPR, Opinion: Morning Edition, December 7, 2005, radio transcript, https://www.npr.org/templates/story/story.php?storyId=5042181.

Chapter 11 When Medicine Fails

1. John O'Donohue, "For a Parent on the Death of a Child," in *To Bless the Space between Us: A Book of Blessings* (New York: Doubleday, 2008), 70.

2. James Russell Lowell, "After the Burial," in *The Poetical Works of James Russell Lowell* (Boston: Houghton Mifflin, 1978), 309.

3. Lowell, "After the Burial," 309.

4. The veracity and true origin of this is disputed: http://www.openculture.com/2015/03/the-urban-legend-of-ernest-hemingways-six-word-story.html.

5. Elise Erickson Barrett, *What Was Lost: A Christian Journey through Miscarriage* (Louisville: Westminster John Knox, 2010), 53.

6. Barrett, *What Was Lost*, 6.

7. L. Serene Jones, "Hope Deferred: Theological Reflections on Reproductive Loss (Infertility, Miscarriage, Stillbirth)," *Modern Theology* 17, no. 2 (April 2001): 231.

8. Alexandra Kimball, "Unpregnant: The Silent, Secret Grief of Miscarriage," *Globe and Mail*, December 3, 2015.

9. Jones, "Hope Deferred," 235.

10. Jones, "Hope Deferred," 241–42.

11. Kimball, "Unpregnant."

12. Brian Doyle, *Book of Uncommon Prayer: 100 Celebrations of the Miracle and Muddle of the Ordinary* (Notre Dame, IN: Sorin Books, 2014), 167.

13. Philip Turner, "Where the Children Can Dance," in *This Incomplete One: Words Occasioned by the Death of a Young Person*, ed. Michael D. Bush (Grand Rapids: Eerdmans, 2006), 157.

14. Annie Proulx, *Fine Just the Way It Is*, Wyoming Stories 3 (New York: Scribner, 2008), 65–66.

15. Joan D. Hedrick, *Harriet Beecher Stowe: A Life* (New York: Oxford University Press, 1994), 191.

16. Edmund Morris, *The Rise of Theodore Roosevelt* (New York: Modern Library, 2001), 230.

17. "Pregnancy Mortality Surveillance System," Centers for Disease Control and Prevention, https://www.cdc.gov/reproductivehealth/maternalinfanthealth/pmss.html; Nina Martin and Renee Montagne, "U.S. Has the Worst Rate of Maternal

Deaths in the Developed World," NPR, May 12, 2017, https://www.npr.org/2017/05/12/528098789/u-s-has-the-worst-rate-of-maternal-deaths-in-the-developed-world.

18. Barrett, *What Was Lost*, 70, cites Luther's "Comfort for Women Who Have Had a Miscarriage," trans. James Raun, in *Luther's Works* (Philadelphia: Fortress, 1968), 43:243–50.

19. Guy Gaucher, *The Story of a Life: St. Thérèse of Lisieux* (San Francisco: HarperCollins, 1987), 197.

20. Turner, "Where the Children Can Dance," 157–59.

21. Turner, "Where the Children Can Dance," 157–59.

Chapter 12 Adoption

1. Kelley Nikondeha, *Adopted: The Sacrament of Belonging in a Fractured World* (Grand Rapids: Eerdmans, 2017), 139.

2. John Irving, *The Cider House Rules* (New York: Bantam, 1986), 72.

3. Read about ZOE in Laceye Warner and Gaston Warner, *From Relief to Empowerment: How Your Church Can Cultivate Sustainable Mission* (Nashville: Wesley's Foundery, 2018).

4. Nikondeha, *Adopted*, 1.

5. Nikondeha, *Adopted*, 4–5.

6. This unsurprising resentment at the broad-scale adoption might find a parallel in the political resentment bubbling up in modern America. Arlie Hochschild explains how so many Americans who've worked hard for generations, who've taken pride in their patriotism and their Christian faith, their clean living and following all the traditional rules feel as if they have been waiting for things to turn their way; but then they see all the newcomers, immigrants, women, refugees, African-Americans, and gays cutting in line ahead of them for benefits, jobs, and privilege. Why do they skip to the front of the line? Who's helping them? Why am I being dissed? See Arlie Russell Hochschild, *Strangers in Their Own Land: Anger and Mourning on the American Right* (New York: New Press, 2016), 137–67.

Chapter 13 Remember Your Baptism

1. Martin Luther, "The Holy and Blessed Sacrament of Baptism," trans. Theodore Bachmann, in *Luther's Works* (Philadelphia: Fortress, 1960), 35:34.

2. Søren Kierkegaard, *Attack upon "Christendom,"* trans. Walter Lowrie (Princeton: Princeton University Press, 1968), 205.

3. Augustine, *On Christian Doctrine*, trans. D. W. Robertson Jr. (Indianapolis: Bobbs-Merrill, 1958), 35–36.

4. Geoffrey Wainwright, *Doxology: The Praise of God in Worship, Doctrine, and Life* (New York: Oxford University Press, 1980), 139.

5. Jürgen Moltmann, *The Church in the Power of the Spirit*, trans. Margaret Kohl (Minneapolis: Fortress, 1993), 235.

6. Rowan Williams, *Being Christian: Baptism, Bible, Eucharist, Prayer* (Grand Rapids: Eerdmans, 2014), 10.

7. P. T. Forsyth, *The Church and the Sacraments* (London: Longmans, Green, 1917), 178, 205; cited in Laurence Hull Stookey, *Baptism: Christ's Act in the Church* (Nashville: Abingdon, 1982), 72.

8. Karl Barth, *Church Dogmatics* IV/4, trans. G. W. Bromiley (Edinburgh: T&T Clark, 1969), 200.

9. Barth, *Church Dogmatics* IV/4, 133, 168; Moltmann, *Church in the Power of the Spirit*, 229.

10. Barth, *Church Dogmatics* IV/4, 186.

11. Alexander Schmemann, *For the Life of the World: Sacraments and Orthodoxy* (Crestwood, NY: St. Vladimir's Seminary Press, 1973), 71.

12. Alex Ross, "The Book of Bach," *New Yorker*, April 11, 2001; cited in Paul Elie, *Reinventing Bach* (New York: Farrar, Straus & Giroux, 2012), 409.

Chapter 14 You Must Be Born Again

1. Arnold A. Dallimore, *George Whitefield: God's Anointed Servant in the Great Revival of the Eighteenth Century* (Wheaton: Crossway, 1990), 12.

2. Stuart C. Henry, *George Whitefield: Wayfaring Witness* (New York: Abingdon, 1957), 22.

3. Dallimore, *George Whitefield*, 17.

4. Henry, *George Whitefield*, 109.

5. Billy Graham, *Just As I Am: The Autobiography of Billy Graham* (New York: HarperCollins, 1997), 487.

6. Graham, *Just As I Am*, 858.

7. John Wesley, *Sermons on Several Occasions* (London: Epworth, 1944), 174.

8. Edgar Young Mullins, *The Christian Religion in Its Doctrinal Expression* (Philadelphia: Roger Williams Press; repr. London: Forgotten Books, 2012), 378.

9. Anne Enright, *Making Babies: Stumbling into Motherhood* (New York: Norton, 2004), 56.

10. C. S. Lewis, *Letters of C. S. Lewis*, ed. W. H. Lewis (New York: Harcourt, Brace & World, 1966), 273.

11. David Wilcox, "Start with the Ending," track 4 on *What You Whispered*, Vanguard Records, 2000.

12. Wesley, *Sermons on Several Occasions*, 518.

13. John Dillenberger, ed., *Martin Luther: Selections from His Writings* (New York: Anchor, 1962), 11.

14. Rudolf Bultmann, *The Gospel of John: A Commentary*, trans. G. R. Beasley-Murray (Philadelphia: Westminster, 1971), 139.

15. Cited with discussion by C. K. Barrett, *The Gospel according to St. John*, 2nd ed. (Philadelphia: Westminster, 1978), 206.

16. Sara Bareilles, "She Used to Be Mine," *Waitress*, premiered August 19, 2015, American Repertory Theatre, Cambridge, MA.

17. Elie Wiesel, *Messengers of God: Biblical Portraits and Legends* (New York: Simon & Schuster, 1976), 32.

18. Ben Witherington III, *John's Wisdom: A Commentary on the Fourth Gospel* (Louisville: Westminster John Knox, 1995), 105.

19. Bultmann, *Gospel of John*, 137.

20. Regis J. Armstrong, J. A. Wayne Hellmann, and William J. Short, eds., *Francis of Assisi: Early Documents* (Hyde Park, NY: New City, 2000), 2:80.

21. Jonathan Wilson-Hartgrove, *Reconstructing the Gospel: Finding Freedom from Slaveholder Religion* (Downers Grove, IL: IVP Books, 2018), 161.

22. R. C. Sproul, *What Does It Mean to Be Born Again?* (Sanford, FL: Reformation Trust, 2010), 2–3.

23. Sproul, *What Does It Mean to Be Born Again?*, 24.

24. Henry, *George Whitefield*, 110.

25. George M. Marsden, *Jonathan Edwards: A Life* (New Haven: Yale University Press, 2003), 160.

26. D. A. Carson, *The Gospel according to John* (Grand Rapids: Eerdmans, 1991), 190.

27. Marianne Meye Thompson, *John: A Commentary* (Louisville: Westminster John Knox, 2015), 81.

28. John O'Donohue, "For a Mother-to-Be," in *To Bless the Space between Us: A Book of Blessings* (New York: Doubleday, 2008), 56.

Scripture Index

Subject and Name Index